Parental Involvement in

Garry Hornby

Parental Involvement in Childhood Education

Building Effective School-Family Partnerships

 Springer

Garry Hornby
College of Education
University of Canterbury
PB 4800
Christchurch 8140
New Zealand
garry.hornby@canterbury.ac.nz

ISBN 978-1-4419-8378-7   e-ISBN 978-1-4419-8379-4
DOI 10.1007/978-1-4419-8379-4
Springer New York Dordrecht Heidelberg London

Library of Congress Control Number: 2011925654

Printed on acid-free paper

Springer is part of Springer Science+Business Media (www.springer.com)

Preface

My aim of writing this book was to provide guidance to school and educational psychologists, and other relevant professionals who work with teachers and schools, on the development of effective practices for facilitating the involvement of parents in the education of their children.

My interest in parental involvement in education emerged when I was teaching adolescents with moderate intellectual disabilities in a secondary school special class in New Zealand 35 years ago. I was advised by another special-class teacher to make home visits early in the school year to all the parents of children in my class. Making these visits helped me build constructive partnerships with most parents, which was of great benefit in teaching their children. However, there were a few parents I could not seem to get through to and so I became aware of not knowing enough about how to work effectively with parents. Later, when I went on to train and work as an educational psychologist, I developed my interest in working with parents further. I began to lead parent education workshops with parents of children with behavioral difficulties and various types of disability and found this very valuable both for the parents and for my understanding of working with them. When I subsequently became a university lecturer and taught courses for trainee and practicing teachers, I have been sure to emphasize the importance of parental involvement and to include sessions on developing the attitudes, knowledge, and skills for working with parents.

After having the above experiences and those of parenting two boys as they have attended elementary, middle, and secondary school, I have come to believe that partnerships between schools and families are essential in providing the optimum education for children. I now consider that developing the relevant skills and knowledge needed for working effectively with parents is essential for all teachers and that developing comprehensive policies and effective practices for parental involvement is essential for all schools.

In this book, I have drawn on these experiences to provide information for psychologists and other professionals who work with schools to help teachers develop the knowledge and skills essential for working effectively with parents and to help schools develop effective policies and practices for parental involvement. I believe that engaging psychologists in this task will help to ensure that the most effective procedures for parental involvement are used by schools to bring about the best possible personal, social, and academic outcomes for children.

Chapter one provides a rationale for the importance of parental involvement and acknowledges the gap between the rhetoric on parental involvement and the reality of its typical practice in schools. The role of psychologists in promoting family–school partnerships and facilitating the involvement of parents in their children's education is considered. Common attitudes of professionals to working with parents are outlined and the attitudes, knowledge, and skills considered to be necessary for working effectively with parents are identified.

Chapter two presents an explanatory model for understanding the various barriers to parental involvement that contribute to the gap between the rhetoric about it and the reality of its practice in schools. Factors related to children, parents and families, parent–teacher relationships, and societal issues are discussed.

Chapter three outlines various approaches to working with parents and presents a model to guide the practice of parental involvement that addresses parents' needs and also their potential contributions. The model is also used to generate a checklist of questions that schools can employ to evaluate their practice of parental involvement to identify strengths and areas that need further development.

Chapter four presents the findings of surveys of the practice of parent involvement in elementary schools in New Zealand, England, and Barbados. It highlights the wide diversity in the practice of parental involvement in the schools and identifies common weaknesses in provision for parental involvement in elementary schools.

Chapter five presents the findings of surveys of the practice of parent involvement in middle and secondary schools in New Zealand, England, and Barbados. Once again, it highlights the wide diversity in parental involvement practices in these schools and identifies common gaps in provision.

Chapter six discusses the strategies for communication with parents that were found useful in schools surveyed about their practice of parental involvement, as reported in Chaps. 4 and 5. These include informal contacts, parent–teacher meetings, different forms of written communication, telephone contacts, home visits, and the use of new technological options such as school websites, e-mail, and text messaging.

Chapter seven outlines the interpersonal skills needed to work effectively with parents, including listening, assertion, and counseling skills, as well as the group leadership skills needed to work with groups of parents.

Chapter eight emphasizes the role that psychologists, and other professionals who work with parents, can play in initiatives to improve parental involvement in the education of their children. It presents an ecological analysis of the key components involved in improving parental involvement, which focuses on changes necessary at the levels of government, education system, school, and teacher.

Acknowledgments

Chapter two is based on the article "Barriers to Parental Involvement In Education: An Explanatory Model," by Garry Hornby and Rayleen Lafaele, published in *Educational Review*, 2011, 63(1), 37–52, with permission.

Chapter four is partly based on the article "Parent Involvement in Rural Elementary Schools in New Zealand: A Survey," by Garry Hornby and Chrystal Witte, published in the *Journal of Child and Family Studies,* 2010, 19(6), 771–777, with permission.

Chapter five is partly based on the article "Parental Involvement in Secondary Schools in New Zealand: Implications for School Psychologists," by Garry Hornby and Chrystal Witte, published in *School Psychology International,* 2010, 31(5), 495–508, with permission.

I would like to thank the following: Chrystal Witte for being my indispensable research associate; John Everatt, Marcia Pilgrim, and David Mitchell for giving me feedback on drafts of the book; my mother-in-law for providing refuge during the time I was putting the book together; my two teenage sons for keeping me grounded in reality throughout the process of producing the book; and the University of Canterbury for providing funds to conduct the studies and present findings at various conferences as well as for providing time to write the book.

About the Author

Garry Hornby (BSc, BA, MA, Dip.Ed.Psych., Ph.D., CPsychol., FBPsS) is a professor of educational psychology in the College of Education at the University of Canterbury in Christchurch, New Zealand. He is a chartered educational and counseling psychologist, and fellow of the British Psychological Society.

Professor Hornby was born in England and completed a degree in physics at the University of Leeds. His first job was as a counselor in a residential school for emotionally disturbed children in the USA. He then worked as a secondary school teacher in England and New Zealand. From there he went on teach a special class for children with moderate learning disabilities, and subsequently, trained and worked as an educational psychologist in Auckland. He worked as a teacher educator at the Auckland College of Education before returning to England to work as a lecturer and researcher at the Universities of Manchester and Hull for 15 years. He lectured for 2 years at the University of the West Indies in Barbados before moving to Christchurch, New Zealand, where he has been for 8 years. He is married to a Barbadian and has two secondary school age sons.

His teaching and research is in the areas of educational psychology, special education, counseling, teacher education, and parental involvement in education. His previous publications include: *Counseling in Child Disability* (Chapman & Hall, 1994), *Improving Parental Involvement* (Cassell, 2000), *Mental Health Handbook for Schools* (Routledge, 2002), *Counseling Pupils in Schools: Skills and Strategies for Teachers* (Routledge, 2003), and *Meeting Special Needs in Mainstream Schools* (2nd ed.) (David Fulton, 2000).

Contents

Chapter 1
Importance of Parental Involvement

Introduction

Extensive international research supports the potential of parental involvement for improving academic achievements and social outcomes for children of all ages (Desforges & Abouchaar, 2003; Epstein, 2001; Jeynes, 2003, 2005, 2007). The most effective schools are now widely considered to be ones that encourage and support the involvement of parents and other family members in the education of their children (Grant & Ray, 2010; Henderson & Mapp, 2002).

Parental involvement is defined as "...parental participation in the educational processes and experiences of their children" (Jeynes, 2005, p. 245). This includes home-based parental involvement, such as listening to children read and supervision of homework, as well as school-based parental involvement, such as attending parent education workshops and parent–teacher meetings. The use of the term "parental" typically denotes any person who is in a parenting role with children. This includes mothers, fathers, grandparents, and other members of the extended family, as well as foster parents and others who are acting as guardians.

The role of parental involvement in improving educational outcomes has been recognized for over 40 years (DES, 1967) and is now acknowledged by governments in many countries. For example, some initiatives that have the role of parental involvement as a key variable in improving educational outcomes are listed below:

- The "No Child Left Behind" policy in the USA (USDoE, 2001), which encouraged the establishment of parent partnerships with schools.
- The "Children's Plan" in the UK (DCSF, 2007), which emphasized the key role of parents in children's education.
- The "Schooling Strategy" in New Zealand (MoE, 2005), which highlights improving parent and family involvement in children's education as one of three priority areas, along with improving the quality of teaching and increasing evidence-based practice.

G. Hornby, *Parental Involvement in Childhood Education: Building Effective School-Family Partnerships*, DOI 10.1007/978-1-4419-8379-4_1,

Extensive evidence for the effectiveness of parental involvement in facilitating children's academic achievement has been reported by several reviews and meta-analyses of the international literature (Cox, 2005; Desforges & Abouchaar, 2003; Fan & Chen, 2001; Henderson & Mapp, 2002; Jeynes, 2005, 2007; Pomerantz, Moorman, & Litwack, 2007). Effect sizes for the impact of parental involvement on children's academic achievement have been calculated from meta-analyses of studies to be 0.51 for all schools (Hattie, 2009), from 0.70 to 0.74 for urban elementary schools (Jeynes, 2005), and from 0.38 to 0.53 for urban secondary schools (Jeynes, 2007). Hattie reports the overall average effect size for educational interventions to be 0.4. This suggests that parental involvement, with effect sizes generally estimated to be larger than this, has a substantial impact on children's academic achievements. So, it is clear that parental involvement has been found to be of considerable importance to children's achievement in schools.

Other merits of parental involvement that emerge from the above reviews encompass benefits for children, teachers, and parents. For children, involvement of their parents is reported to lead to improvements in children's attitudes, behavior, and attendance at school, as well as in their mental health. For teachers, effective parental involvement is reported to improve parent–teacher relationships, teacher morale, and the school climate. For parents, involvement in their children's education has been linked to increased parental confidence in and satisfaction with parenting, as well as increased interest in their own education. Other important findings from these reviews are that the effectiveness of parental involvement in bringing about these changes applies across gender and ethnic groups and that this also applies across the age range, including children at elementary, middle, and secondary schools.

Despite widespread acknowledgement of these potential benefits, however, there are clear gaps between the rhetoric on parental involvement found in the literature and typical parental involvement practices found in schools. As stated by Christenson and Sheridan (2001) "…there is still more rhetoric than reality about family and school working together as genuine partners" (p. 18). This view is supported by the findings of two surveys. First, a survey of secondary school teachers in the USA found that 83% of teachers considered that the level of parental involvement in their schools should be increased (Binns, Steinberg, & Amorosi, 1997). Second, a survey of parents in the UK reported that 72% of mothers wanted more involvement in their children's education (Williams, Williams, & Ullman, 2002).

In addition, Grant and Ray (2010) make the point that many forms of parental involvement traditionally used by schools are of more benefit to teachers and schools than they are to parents and families. Activities such as fund-raising, attending PTA meetings, or providing voluntary help in the classroom have long been engaged in by parents and are easily accepted by schools. But for parental involvement to be optimally effective, it is important to not only focus on such activities but also emphasize other aspects that are part of a true partnership between schools and parents, such as productive parent–teacher meetings and effective two-way communication.

Role of Psychologists in Parental Involvement

School and educational psychologists working in many countries around the world have long been aware of the importance of facilitating parental involvement in children's education (Jimmerson, Oakland, & Farrell, 2006; Koutrouba, Antonopoulou, Tsitsas, & Zenakou, 2009). Assisting teachers and schools to develop effective strategies for parent involvement is an important role for professionals who work with schools, especially school psychologists. There have been two studies, conducted in USA, which are particularly relevant to the roles that psychologists can play in facilitating effective parental involvement in schools. Both studies emphasize the important leadership role that psychologists can play in helping schools develop effective strategies for parental involvement.

In the first study, Christenson, Hurley, Sheridan, and Fensternmacher (1997) surveyed 217 parents on the extent to which they believed schools should offer, and they would use, 33 different parental involvement activities. They also surveyed 409 school psychologists on the feasibility of schools implementing these 33 activities. These researchers found that the activities that parents reported they were most likely to use were ones that psychologists rated as being the most feasible for schools to implement. In particular, there was agreement on psychologists' ratings of 8 of the top 11 activities rated by parents, most of which focused on providing parents with information on how schools functioned, on children's development, on how to help their children at home, and about community resources available.

In the second study, Pelco, Ries, Jacobson, and Melka (2000) surveyed 417 school psychologists to obtain responses to five questions about their perspectives of parental involvement and their involvement in 12 types of parental involvement activities. Results showed that psychologists were very positive about the value of parental involvement and believed that it was important for them to be actively involved in supporting the implementation of parental involvement in the schools in which they worked. Highly rated activities included consulting with families about ways to support their children's learning and behavior at school, helping schools develop methods of communicating with families, and, providing in-service training to professionals on ways to involve parents in children's schoolwork.

Pelco et al. (2000) have suggested that psychologists have a key role to play in the in-service training of professionals, such as teachers, for parental involvement. For example, psychologists can help professionals develop effective communication skills for use with parents, as well as techniques for organizing effective parent–teacher conferences. Psychologists can also encourage professionals to make home visits to families who would appreciate this. In addition to their training and guidance of professionals, psychologists can work with parents of children at all ages to ensure that they have the information they need to use effective home-based parental involvement activities and for collaborating effectively with schools. For example, psychologists can help parents develop strategies for conveying higher educational aspirations to their children. Psychologists can also encourage the involvement of extended family members in home-based and school-based parental involvement. Pelco et al. made the point that psychologists must advocate for parental involvement programs that schools have developed themselves and are integral to their educational mission, rather than short-term, add-on programs, since these are likely to be less effective. In these ways, psychologists have a key role to play in promoting family–school partnerships and facilitating overall parental involvement in the education of children.

Attitudes of Professionals Toward Parents

The gap between rhetoric and reality regarding parental involvement in their children's education has long been considered to be at least partly due to limitations posed by attitudes that professionals, such as psychologists and teachers, often have toward parents. If professionals do exhibit some negative attitudes toward parents, then it is hardly surprising since the majority of them would have received little or no input on working with parents on their initial training courses or as a part of any subsequent in-service training. Their attitudes toward parents would, therefore, have been influenced by those of senior colleagues and their own experiences of education. Research conducted with teachers indicates that they typically find interactions with parents to be a major source of stress in their jobs (Turnbull & Turnbull, 1986). On the other side of the fence, parents are often reported to find communications with professionals such as teachers to be equally stressful. It is therefore important to identify the attitudes toward parents that are commonly held by professionals and which get in the way of the development of effective parental involvement.

Common Attitudes Toward Parents

It has been suggested that certain common attitudes that many professionals hold toward parents can contribute substantially toward the stress caused by their relationships with one another (Sonnenschien, 1984). These include the fact that parents are often viewed as being either problems or adversaries. Alternatively, they are seen as vulnerable, less able, or in need of treatment themselves. In addition, parents are sometimes considered to be the cause of their children's problems. Finally, for various reasons, perhaps related to the above views, many professionals, such as teachers and psychologists, adopt an attitude of "professional distance". These common attitudes toward parents are discussed below, followed by discussion of attitudes that are more conducive to the development of effective working relationships with parents.

Parents as Problems

Some professionals who work in the field of education see parents mainly as problems. When parents are convinced that there is something wrong with their child despite reassurance from professionals, they are considered to be "overanxious." When parents disagree with a diagnosis, or the results of an assessment, and ask for a second opinion, they are said to be "denying the reality" of the situation. When parents refuse to accept the educational programs or placements suggested for their child, and are adamant about what they want, they are regarded as being "aggressive." Viewing parents in these ways makes it difficult to develop productive working relationships with them.

Parents as Adversaries

There is a tendency for professionals, especially teachers, to view parents as adversaries. Professionals may have different goals and priorities to parents concerning the educational programs suggested for their children. This can create conflict and sometimes competition between parents and professionals. Competition can also be focused on children's achievements. For example, children will typically behave more appropriately for their teachers than they will for their parents. In contrast, parents often report that children do things at home that are not observed at school. In these situations, it is easy for either teachers or parents to feel doubtful or resentful about the others' success in getting the child to perform well. However, avoiding the tendency to view parents as adversaries is essential for the development of good relationships.

Parents as Vulnerable

Professionals may regard parents as being too vulnerable to be treated as equal partners. This occurs most often when professionals are reluctant to tell parents the whole truth about their child's difficulties in case they become upset. So, some of the child's weaknesses may be glossed over or parents may be given an overly optimistic view of their child's likely future progress. This does not promote the development of good relationships since parents are widely reported to appreciate professionals telling them all that they know about the child's difficulties as honestly as possible. Alternatively, professionals who come across as superior will actually contribute to feelings of vulnerability in parents, which may lead them to become defensive and resistant to suggestions. Feeling vulnerable is an understandable reaction in parents who are seeking help for their child. Therefore, professionals should strive to allay this feeling, not add to it, as they sometimes unintentionally do, by developing the skills necessary for communicating sensitively and effectively with parents.

Parents as Less Able

There is a tendency for parents to be viewed as less observant, less perceptive, and less intelligent than professionals. Therefore, parents' ideas and opinions are not given the credence that they deserve. This is a pity since most parents have an abundance of information about their children that can be invaluable to the professionals who work with them, especially their teachers. A more helpful view is to consider that while professionals such as psychologists and teachers are the experts on child development and education, parents are the experts on their children.

Parents as Needing Treatment

Some professionals believe that many parents who have children with problems find this difficult to accept and therefore are in need of counseling. This assumed weakness in parents then becomes the focus of attention rather than the child. Such views are experienced as patronizing and extremely frustrating by parents. It is therefore unwise to make assumptions about possible difficulties that parents may have. It is generally more helpful for the development of productive relationships when professionals focus on parents' strengths rather than their weaknesses.

Parents as Causal

Another possible attitudinal barrier to developing effective working relationships with parents occurs when professionals consider that parents have caused or contributed to children's problems. This tends to happen more with children who have emotional or behavioral difficulties. These are often considered by professionals to be caused by parents who have deprived their children of love or discipline. Even with children who have learning difficulties, there is a tendency to assume that these have been made worse by poor parenting. Many parents who have children with difficulties or disabilities experience guilt for one reason or another. Some wonder whether they are in any way responsible for causing the problems, while others feel guilty about not being able to spend more time working with their children to overcome their difficulties. Therefore, it is of no benefit for professionals to add to these guilt feelings by communicating to parents, either indirectly or directly their views about the parents' role in causing their children's problems.

Parents Needing to Be Kept at a "Professional Distance"

Many psychologists and teachers prefer to keep parents at a professional distance. They do not want to establish close working relationships with parents in case this causes problems. This attitude can result from professionals subscribing to any of the negative attitudes discussed above or can be due to a lack of confidence about being able to relate well to parents. Also, the necessity for emotional distance to be maintained between professionals and their clients is an attitude that in the past has been encouraged in many professional training courses. Unfortunately, parents perceive this emotional distance as being indicative of the lack of empathy professionals have with their situation. Therefore, they typically have little confidence in any professionals who operate at such a professional distance.

Attitudes Needed to Work Effectively with Parents

In contrast to the negative views of parents that are described above, the attitudes that professionals need to work effectively with parents are widely considered to be ones that will help them develop productive working relationships. To bring this about, professionals need to communicate to parents the attitudes of *genuineness*, *respect*, and *empathy* suggested by Carl Rogers (1980). They must be *genuine* in their relationships with parents. That is, they should come across as real people with their own strengths and weaknesses. For example, they should always be prepared to say that they "don't know" when it is the case. Hiding behind a professional facade of competence is not in anyone's interest. Professionals also need to show *respect* for parents. Parents' opinions and requests should always be given serious consideration, and in most cases parents' wishes should be respected even if they run counter to the views of professionals, since it is parents who have the long-term responsibility for their children. Most importantly, professionals need to develop *empathy* with parents. They should try to see the child's situation from the parent's point of view. If professionals can develop an empathic understanding of the parent's position, then it is much more likely that a productive parent–professional partnership will evolve.

Another important attitude that professionals, such as teachers and psychologists, need to have is hopeful but realistic views about the likely progress of the children with whom they work. Parents need professionals to be optimistic but objective about their children's development. They need professionals to be people of integrity who will not shy away from being open and honest with them about their children's strengths and weaknesses, but will do this with sensitivity.

Competencies Needed to Work Effectively with Parents

In addition to communicating appropriate attitudes, to work effectively with parents, professionals who work with them, such as psychologists, social workers, counselors, and teachers, need to have specific skills and knowledge. These are outlined below and expanded on in later chapters of the book.

Skills Needed to Work Effectively with Parents

In order to work effectively with parents, professionals need to have a range of relevant skills. Teachers in particular need the organizational and communication skills necessary for maintaining contact with parents through such means as meetings, written communication, home visits, and telephone calls. These forms of contact are discussed in Chap. 6. All professionals who work with parents need to have a high level of listening and counseling skills to be able to deal with problems or concerns raised by parents. Other interpersonal skills required by professionals include the assertion skills needed for working with parents and for collaborating with colleagues who are working with the same children, families, and schools. In addition, it is useful for psychologists, counselors, and teachers to develop the skills required for organizing groups with parents, especially those needed for leading parent education workshops. Listening, counseling and assertion skills, as well as the skills required for working with groups of parents are discussed in Chap. 7.

Knowledge Needed to Work Effectively with Parents

In the past 30 years, there has been a substantial growth in the number of publications on parental involvement, and there are now a large number of books and articles on the topic, which provide information for professionals on how to implement effective parental involvement (e.g. Blank & Kershaw, 1998; Boult, 2006; Grant & Ray, 2010; Henderson, Mapp, Johnson, & Davies, 2007; Hornby, 2000; Turnbull, Turnbull, Erwin, Soodak, & Shogren, 2011). One aim of this book is to highlight, from this literature, the essential knowledge required by professionals to work effectively with parents. There are several aspects of this knowledge.

First and foremost, professionals, such as teachers, psychologists, and counselors who work in schools, must have a thorough understanding of the various barriers to parental involvement. These are related to child, family, parent–teacher, and societal factors and are discussed in Chap. 2. Professionals must also have a good knowledge of strategies and techniques needed for improving the parental involvement organized by schools, which includes such things as guidelines for meetings and other activities involving parents, as well as guidelines for organizing parent education workshops (Boult, 2006; Grant & Ray, 2010; Hornby, 2000). They need to have a good understanding of parents' perspectives, that is, they must be able to see and appreciate parents' points of view. Professionals must also be aware of family dynamics and be able to view all children within the context of their families (Bronfenbrenner, 1979). In addition, professionals need to know specifically what they can do to help parents of children with various types of difficulties, such as those with disabilities and illnesses as well as children affected by bereavement and family breakdown (see Hornby, 1995, 2000). Professionals also need to have adequate knowledge of how to work effectively with parents who themselves present particular challenges, such as being too aggressive or overprotective of their children (see Hornby, 2000). Professionals need to be knowledgeable about the range of services and other resources that are available to parents. They need to be sufficiently aware of the beliefs and customs of the ethnic groups with which they work to ensure that their working relationships are culturally appropriate (Grant & Ray, 2011).

Model Needed to Work Effectively with Parents

When working as an educational psychologist in New Zealand around 20 years ago, I came to the conclusion that it is also important for professionals to have a theoretical model for parental involvement. This provides them with a framework for helping schools to develop a comprehensive range of activities for involving parents in their children's education. I therefore developed a model that combines the elements of a number of theories of parental involvement and creates a framework that includes both parental contributions and parental needs (Hornby, 1990). The model includes four types of activities focusing on parental contributions: policy formation, acting as a resource, collaborating with teachers, and sharing information on children. The model also includes four types of activities focusing on parental needs: channels of communication, liaison with school staff, parent education, and, parent support. Full details of the model are presented in Chap. 3. I have subsequently used the model in workshops and courses for trainee and practicing professionals, including teachers, social workers, counselors, and psychologists working in education for the past 20 years. However, until recently, I have not had the opportunity to use the model to investigate the practice of parental involvement in schools. Recently, studies using the model as a survey framework have been conducted in elementary, middle, and high schools. The findings of these studies are reported in Chaps. 4 and 5. But before going on to present the model, and report on the research carried out in schools using it, it is important to clarify the various factors that act as barriers to developing meaningful partnerships with parents and thereby to schools implementing effective parental involvement. Without a thorough appreciation of these barriers, it is not possible for professionals to fully understand what is necessary to develop effective parental involvement.

Summary and Conclusion

A rationale is presented for the importance of parental involvement in the education of their children, and the evidence for its effectiveness in facilitating children's academic achievements is summarized. The gap between the rhetoric on parental involvement and the reality of its typical practice in schools is noted. The role of psychologists in promoting family–school partnerships and facilitating parental involvement overall is considered. Common attitudes of professionals to working with parents are outlined, and the attitudes, knowledge, and skills considered to be necessary for working effectively with parents are identified. It was concluded that professionals, such as psychologists, who work with parents need a theoretical model to guide their practice, which is the focus of Chap. 3. They also need a thorough understanding of the various barriers to implementing effective parental involvement, which is the focus of the chapter that follows.

Chapter 2
Barriers to Parental Involvement[*]

Introduction

As can be seen from Chap. 1, the literature on the involvement of parents in the education of their children encompasses extensive research indicating its effectiveness, the reported value given to it by both educators and parents, and a substantial collection of theoretical models and publications providing guidance about its implementation. The reality of parental involvement is, however, quite different. Henderson and Berla (1994) summarized the situation succinctly when they stated, "The benefits of effective collaborations and how to do them are well documented across all the age ranges of schooling. Still they are not in widespread practice" (p. 18). Sixteen years later, this situation has not substantially changed. The current reality is that there is considerable diversity in the type and degree of parental involvement, with modal practice being at the more traditional end of the spectrum that focuses on a one directional flow of support from parents to schools. The typical approach to parental involvement reflects a lack of understanding, guiding framework, and professional training, which not surprisingly results in variable effectiveness (Hornby, 2000; Lueder, 2000; Pomerantz, Moorman, & Litwack, 2007).

This chapter addresses the lack of understanding of key issues regarding parental involvement. It is proposed that there are many reasons for the gap between what is said and what is done in the name of parental involvement and these can be conceptualized as barriers to such involvement. The various barriers to parental involvement can be categorized by adapting Epstein's (2001) framework of overlapping spheres of influence focused on the three areas of family, school, and community. For the purpose of discussion in this chapter, these three spheres of influence have been adapted to become broader societal factors, which influence the functioning of both schools and families, parent–teacher factors, individual parent and family factors, and an additional focus on child factors. The chapter presents a model that has been developed in order to clarify and elaborate on the barriers in each of

---

[*]Also contributed to by Rayleen Lafaele.

G. Hornby, *Parental Involvement in Childhood Education: Building Effective School-Family Partnerships*, DOI 10.1007/978-1-4419-8379-4_2,

Individual parent and family factors	Child factors
• parents' beliefs about PI	• age
• perceptions of invitations for PI	• learning difficulties and disabilities
• current life contexts	• gifts and talents
• class, ethnicity and gender	• behavioural problems

Parent-teacher factors	Societal factors
• differing goals and agendas	• historical & demographic
• differing attitudes	• political
• differing language used	• economic

Fig. 2.1 Model of factors acting as barriers to parental involvement (PI)

these four areas (see Fig. 2.1). These barriers to the establishment of effective parental involvement in education are discussed below. First, individual parent and family barriers are discussed, focusing on parents' beliefs about parental involvement, parents' current life contexts, parents' perceptions of invitations for involvement, and class, ethnicity, and gender. Next, child factors are addressed focusing on age, learning difficulties and disabilities, gifts and talents, and behavioral problems. Then, parent–teacher factors are discussed, focusing on differing agendas, attitudes, and language used. Finally, societal factors are elaborated on, including historical and demographic issues, political issues, and economic issues.

Parent and Family Factors

Parents' Beliefs About Parental Involvement

Parents' beliefs about various issues can act as barriers to effective parental involvement. First, the way that parents view their role in their children's education is crucial. Parents who believe that their role is only to get children to school, which then takes over responsibility for their education, will not be willing to be actively involved in either school-based or home-based parental involvement. Hoover-Dempsey and Sandler (1997) reported that this attitude is more prevalent in some communities and national cultures than others but that there is considerable variation within these. For example, Clark (1983), in his research on high-achieving students from low-income black families, found that what distinguished the parents of these students from others at the school was that they believed that they should be involved in their children's education, by both supporting their learning at home and interacting constructively with schools. Clark found that parents of high achieving students had a greater belief than the other parents that they could effectively help their children to do better at school.

The belief that parents have in their own ability to help their children succeed at school is the second belief that is crucial to parental involvement. Hoover-Dempsey and Sandler (1997) point out that parents with a low level of belief in their ability to help their children are likely to avoid contact with schools because of their view that such involvement will not bring about positive outcomes for their children. For some parents, lack of confidence in helping their children may be because the language of instruction is not their first language and they feel they cannot communicate effectively with teachers. For others, it can come from them having had negative experiences with their children's previous schools, or through them experiencing either learning or behavioral difficulties during their own schooling. Lack of confidence may also come from parents taking the view that they have not developed sufficient academic competence to effectively help their children. This view is more apparent as students progress through secondary schools and their academic work becomes more advanced (Eccles & Harold, 1993). Such views act as a barrier to parental involvement, despite widespread acknowledgement that the ability to support children's learning does not require a high level of education from parents (Clark, 1983; Hoover-Dempsey & Sandler; Hornby, 2000).

The third type of parental beliefs that are critical to involvement in their children's education are parents' views about children's intelligence, as well as how children learn and develop their abilities (Hoover-Dempsey & Sandler, 1997). Parents who believe that children's intelligence is fixed, and that school achievement is mainly due to children being lucky enough to have high ability, will not see the point in getting too involved in their children's education. They believe that children's innate ability will set a limit on their achievement so that such things as encouraging children to do their homework or attending parent–teacher meetings at school are viewed as a waste of time. Alternatively, parents who believe that achievement at school depends as much on effort as ability, and that children's abilities can always be developed, are more likely to be positive about parental involvement. Related to this are parents' beliefs about the role they should play in supporting this development, in fact their beliefs about child rearing in general (Hoover-Dempsey & Sandler). Parents who believe that the way they bring up their children will have considerable impact on their development are much more likely to be positive about parental involvement than parents who believe they can have little impact on their children's development.

Parents' Perceptions of Invitations for Involvement

Another potential barrier to parental involvement is parents' perceptions of the level of explicit and implicit invitations for involvement. When parents think that parental involvement is not valued by teachers or schools, they are less likely to get involved (Hoover-Dempsey & Sandler, 1997). Therefore, parents' perceptions of invitations from schools are considered crucial in developing effective parental involvement. Epstein (2001) has found that parents are most effectively involved when teachers actively encourage this. Teachers with positive, facilitating attitudes toward involving parents encourage more parents to become involved and increase the effectiveness of parental involvement (Eccles & Harold, 1993). When parents perceive that teachers are not open to involving parents, this acts as a major barrier to their involvement. Similarly, schools that are welcoming to parents, and make it clear that they value parental involvement, develop more effective practices than schools that do not appear inviting to parents. Secondary schools are often seen by parents as large bureaucratic organizations that are not welcoming to parents, which is considered to be one of the reasons why there is a tendency for higher levels of parental involvement in primary than secondary schools (Eccles & Harold).

Parents' Current Life Contexts

Several aspects of parents' life contexts can act as barriers to parental involvement. Parents' level of education will influence their views on whether they have sufficient skills and knowledge to engage in different aspects of parental involvement (Green, Walker, Hoover-Dempsey, & Sandler, 2007). For example, parents who did not complete high school may be diffident about helping their children with homework once they get to secondary school. Also, parents without university degrees may feel in some ways inferior to teachers who they know are better qualified than them and therefore may be diffident about meeting with teachers.

Family circumstances can be major barriers to parental involvement. For example, solo parents and those with young families or large families may find it more difficult to get involved in their children's education because of their caretaking responsibilities. Parents' work situations can also be a factor. When parents are unemployed, money could be an issue, as they may not be able to afford a car or to pay babysitters to get to school meetings. For parents with jobs, whether both parents work and the kind of jobs they have may be issues. When both parents work, there will be less time available for both home-based and school-based parental involvement. Also, while some jobs allow little flexibility for taking time off for school-based parental involvement, other jobs may leave parents too tired at the end of the day to help children with homework (Catsambis, 2001; Green et al., 2007).

Finally, parents' overall psychological resources may be a barrier to parental involvement. For example, parents with poor physical or mental health or without an effective social support network, including extended family members, may find it difficult to engage effectively in their children's education (Eccles & Harold, 1993).

Class, Ethnicity, and Gender

There are also barriers relating to class, ethnicity, and gender of parents that are relevant when accounting for the gap between rhetoric and reality in parental involvement. Differences in class, ethnicity, and gender may play a role in determining the degree to which parents are involved with schools (OECD, 1997). While the rhetoric on parental involvement does include suggestions of how to overcome the typical disadvantages of social class and ethnicity, it does so with an essential bias of white middle-class values that ignores difference and diversity. It is a rhetoric of parental involvement that benefits, and is committed to, a dominant white middle-class involvement which, unsurprisingly, is precisely the group of parents who are the main participants in such involvement (Bastianai, 1989). Those largely involved are, as defined by teachers, the "good parents" who typically are white middle-class, married, and heterosexual (Reay, 1998).

Reay (1998) suggests that it is these parents who possess cultural capital that matches that generally valued by schools. In contrast, working-class parents are aware of the difference between the cultural capital they possess and that of teachers. Reay concludes that, for working-class families, home–school relationships are about separateness, whereas for middle-class families they are about interconnectedness, and this difference shapes their respective attitudes to parental involvement. In general, minorities are less involved, less represented and less informed, and are less likely to have access to resources, as well as more likely to have problems associated with language, transport, communication, and child care. They have substantially different relationships with teachers, who most often share white middle-class cultural capital (OECD, 1997). In comparison, white middle-class parents face no such obstacles in becoming involved at school. They have the resources and power to enable them to continue to seek advantages for their own children, for example, by engaging home-help to free up time for greater involvement at school. This type of class-related parental involvement helps maintain the current inequalities in the system and the gap between rhetoric and reality (Reay).

Barriers related to ethnicity and culture are also important. A report by Koki and Lee (1998) explains some of the issues involved in parental involvement for parents in New Zealand who have come from the Pacific Islands. They make the point that it is impossible to understand these issues outside of the context of the history of Pacific education and cultural tradition, but the reality is that parental involvement programs typically pay scant regard to these issues. For example, there is a general lack of knowledge about how to capitalize on Pacific cultural background positively when trying to involve parents. Within these cultures, there is a significant emphasis on titles and social class, with an understanding that lineage and culture are family domains. Since education is considered the domain of schools, parental involvement will remain limited, unless it is supported by community and church leaders (Koki & Lee).

In another study, Young (1998) examined the impact of cultural issues in the development of trust between Mexican-American parents and schools in the USA.

The study found that the "existence or absence of trust between the home and the school affects the development and sustenance of meaningful parental involvement" (Young, 1998, p. 1). Young's finding that cultural roles, expectations, and values play a pivotal part in how trust is perceived and developed is further evidence of the need to be aware of the context of culture and ethnicity. Failure to understand the impact of ethnicity on parental involvement and to incorporate programs that are genuinely inclusive of other cultures is probably another reason why the practice of involving parents in schools is typically less effective than it could be.

It is also significant that despite policy and research supporting the importance of parental involvement in schools, the term itself is a misnomer because, as Reay (1998) points out, the reality is that it is predominantly mothers' involvement. Since most of the rhetoric and research ignores the issue of the gendered nature of parental involvement, it also fails to consider and evaluate its impact on practice. However, analysis of the "mother's world" does clearly show that there are tensions and compromises involved in determining levels of parental involvement. The involvement of many mothers is heavily influenced by their family-focused lives, and this context puts constraints on how they respond to and interact with educators and educational systems. Their view of educational issues is often vastly different to that of educationalists since it is concerned with a holistic focus on the family unit (David, Edwards, Hughes, & Ribbens, 1993).

There have also been significant changes over the past few decades in family structures, and in the political, economic, and historical context in which mothers' involvement occurs. Now, mothers face balancing issues of working with schools, increased workload, and participation in the labor market, as well as the effects of class, marital status, and ethnicity. These issues contribute to the reasons for the discrepancy between the rhetoric and typical practice of parental involvement.

Child Factors

Age of Children

The age of children can be a barrier to the involvement of parents, since it is widely acknowledged that parental involvement decreases as children grow older and is at its lowest level for children of secondary school age. The tendency for greater involvement of parents of younger children may be partly because younger children are more positive about their parents going into school. Whereas, older children are less keen about school involvement, such as parents going on class trips, which is at least partly due to adolescents wanting to become independent of their parents (Eccles & Harold, 1993). However, adolescents are still considered to desire and benefit from their parents being involved in other ways, such as helping them with homework and making subject choices. Deslandes and Cloutier (2002) found, in their study of 872 fourteen-year-old children in the USA, that over three quarters of these adolescents were willing to show their parents what they learned or did well on at school, ask parents for ideas for projects, listen to parents tell them about when they were teenagers, and take home notes, notices, and newsletters. Also, in their study of children's perspectives on parental involvement, Edwards and Alldred (2000) found that children referred to far more involvement of their parents occurring in the home setting than at school. In spite of these findings, parents, and sometimes teachers, can misinterpret the situation and assume that older children do not want parents to be involved in their education, which can act as a barrier to effective parental involvement.

Learning Difficulties and Disabilities

Children's performance at school can be a barrier or facilitating factor for parental involvement. When children are struggling with their schoolwork due to learning difficulties or disabilities, parents are generally more inclined to be active in parental involvement activities (Eccles & Harold, 1993). In fact, many authorities on special needs education consider that involving parents is an essential aspect of effective education for children with disabilities or learning difficulties (Hornby, 1995; Seligman, 2000). Because the involvement of parents is required for the process of implementing individual education programs, this facilitates the involvement of many parents of children with learning difficulties or disabilities. However, this is not always the case, since there are many possible areas for disagreement between schools and parents of children with learning difficulties or disabilities which can act as barriers to effective involvement, for example, when parents consider that their children can achieve more academically or when teachers want more support from parents in backing up at home what children are working on at school (Seligman).

Gifts and Talents

For children who are doing well at school, it is usually a pleasure for parents to attend parent–teacher meetings, so children being gifted or talented is usually a facilitating factor for parental involvement. However, barriers to effective parental involvement can be evident when parents consider their children are academically gifted if this view is not shared by teachers (Montgomery, 2009). Parents in this situation tend to lose confidence in the school and therefore reduce their involvement with teachers. Also, many children who are academically gifted become frustrated at school, typically because they are being insufficiently challenged, and either begin to underachieve or develop behavior problems. Either situation is likely to lead to conflict between parents and teachers, which then acts as a barrier to effective involvement of parents.

There is also potential for conflict between teachers and parents of children who are talented in extracurricular areas such as sport or musical abilities.

Developing their talents in these areas demands that children put in a lot of time and effort practicing or competing, which often requires them to take time off school and can lead them to get behind with their academic studies. Schools vary in how understanding they are of the needs of such children, and when parents consider that schools are not responsive to the extracurricular demands on their children it can prove to be a barrier to positive parental involvement.

Behavioral Problems

When children develop a reputation for exhibiting challenging behavior their parents can be reluctant to go into schools for fear of getting more bad news. In fact, there is usually a negative correlation between parental involvement and children's behavior problems, such that the more disruptive the behavior, the less parents are inclined to be involved with the school. When behavior problems become so severe that schools begin to consider suspension or expulsion, conflict between schools and parents is almost inevitable and presents a formidable barrier to meaningful parental involvement (Parsons, 1999).

Parent–Teacher Factors

Goals and Agendas

Related to the parent and child factors discussed above is the issue of differences in goals and agendas between families and schools involved in making home–school alliances a reality. Parent and teacher interactions and roles are frequently shaped by differing expectations and vested interests (Wolfendale, 1983). The parental involvement rhetoric that exists is not merely a function of a simplistic desire to benefit children, but also the result of these differing and sometimes opposing goals and agendas. For example, governments and schools may, from the perspective of their goals, see parental involvement as a tool for increasing school accountability to their communities and for increasing children's achievements, or as a cost-effective resource, as well as a method of addressing cultural disadvantage and inequality. On the contrary, parents' goals are more likely to be focused on improving their children's performance, wishing to influence the ethos or curriculum within the school, and wanting to increase their understanding of school life (OECD, 1997). Teachers also have their own goals for parental involvement, as is illustrated by Rudney (2005) who reports that the focus of teachers is on parental involvement in the areas of homework, providing a nurturing environment, fund-raising, as well as attending school events and parent–teacher meetings.

Parent–teacher meetings provide a good example of how much the goals and agendas of parents and teachers can differ. Bastiani (1989) has suggested that teachers' goals for parent–teacher meetings include discussing children's progress and any difficulties they are having, finding out from parents how children are coping with school, identifying ways in which parents can help their children at home, and identifying potential conflicts with parents. Parents goals for parent–teacher meetings include discussing children's progress and any difficulties they are having, comparing their children's progress with that of others in the class, learning more about the school and methods of teaching used, and questioning teachers about any concerns they have (Bastiani). So, it is clear that although there are similarities, there are also important differences in parents' and teachers' agendas for these meetings, which act as barriers to the establishment of effective parental involvement.

Adelman (1992), in discussing the impact of these differing goals, considers that home–school relationships are based upon an agenda of socialization, where schools attempt to shape parental attitudes and practices so that they facilitate schooling. He suggests that models and rhetoric concerning parental involvement often have underlying agendas that are largely concerned with meeting the needs of the school or society. So, it is possible to differentiate the many different types of parental involvement according to whether they are about improving individuals or the school (Adelman). These differences in goals create conflicts that limit the type and success of parental involvement practices and result in frustration as each party seeks to maximize its own agenda, independent of, and often in opposition to that of the others. Understanding these underlying and typically covert agendas provides an example of the influence of the complex context in which parental involvement occurs.

Attitudes

Another critical factor in understanding the complexity of the difference between what is said and what is done with regard to parental involvement is the attitudes of parents and teachers. It is at this level that the impact of many of the other factors already discussed becomes evident. Teachers and parents each bring to the melting pot of parental involvement personal attitudes that are deeply rooted within their own historical, economic, educational, ethnic, class, and gendered experiences. There persists among many teachers a deficit model of parents that is manifested through attitudes whereby parents are viewed as "problems," "vulnerable," or "less able" and are therefore best kept out of schools (see Chap. 1). However, within the context of the new neoliberal market-driven economy, where parents are often constructed as consumers, parental attitudes have changed from ones of deference and helplessness to a recognition of their rights (Bastiani, 1993). Nonetheless, as Bastiani states, "parents speak with many voices" (as cited in Waller & Waller, 1998, p. 113), and they are far from being a homogeneous group, generally lacking clear agendas, and possessing little political power (Munn, 1993).

At a fundamental level, parents and teachers may also differ in their understanding of the relationship between schooling and education. If education is largely about schooling, then logically it is teachers that possess the greatest knowledge, skills, and expertise. If, however, schooling is merely a part of education, then there is a clear shift in power and expertise toward parents, who are intimately involved in the other 85% of children's education, which occurs outside of school (Munn, 1993). To put it succinctly, "Should school teachers educate children while parents humbly support the schools? Or ... Are parents the main educators of their child, while schools supplement home-learning with specialist expertise?" (OECD, 1997, p. 52). Clearly, differing attitudes on this point will have major repercussions for how parental involvement is perceived, structured, valued, and, most importantly, how it is implemented.

There are many assumptions made about parents, including a pervasive notion that they are increasingly not meeting their responsibilities nowadays, as was done in the past. Whereas, research findings suggest that parent–child relationships are increasingly more loving, that child health has improved, and that abuse once tolerated is no longer accepted (Rudney, 2005; Waller & Waller, 1998; Wolfendale, 1983). However, media and television constantly highlight negative examples of parenting and often portray parents as weak, incompetent, and besieged by problems. Many teachers make assumptions that some parents are not interested or do not really care about their children's education. Whereas, parents often feel ignorant of the curriculum and processes of schools. They may believe that teachers are seeking a superficial relationship and are only concerned with focusing on problems rather than working toward solutions. In this context, it is not surprising that there is a lack of mutual understanding between parents and teachers, with the result that mistrust builds and barriers increase.

It is widely accepted that the vast majority of parents do care about their children's education and that working-class parents care just as much as middle-class parents (Epstein, 2001; Wolfendale, 1983). Further, most teachers are genuine in their desire to actually find solutions and to engage meaningfully with parents. Teachers are nowadays, however, working in an environment where they are increasingly held accountable for children's achievements (e.g., through the publication of the results of national tests) and are often required to assume responsibility for tasks for which they have received little or no training, including working closely with parents (OECD, 1997). The result is that the differences between the assumptions held by parents and teachers contribute to the gap between the rhetoric and reality of parental involvement. This differences in assumptions and the disparity between the goals of parents and teachers can result in poorly planned attempts to increase parental involvement, which may result in parents and teachers being pushed further apart, thereby increasing distrust (Waller & Waller, 1998).

A comparison of two studies of parent and teacher attitudes illustrates the depth and breadth of the attitudinal obstacles that play such a central part in the gap between reality and rhetoric in parental involvement. First, a parental attitude survey conducted by the National Opinion Research Centre (1997) in the USA shows that parents believe overwhelmingly that schools see them as being valuable for their child's learning and that they want both themselves and teachers to learn more about ways they can be involved in schools. Parents wanted more involvement, particularly in the area of academics and decision making. Second, an investigation into teacher perceptions shows that they have quite specific ideas about the type, frequency, and the nature of the involvement that they want from parents (Baker, 1997). The participants in this study expressed a desire that parents support their ideas and efforts and, although recognizing that parents face some barriers, they expressed a belief that, if parents really wanted, they could find ways to be more involved. They saw support of homework as being very important along with the need for parents to care properly for their children physically and emotionally. They believed parents to be good resources of skills, talents, and funds, but also often saw them as questioning their professionalism.

Language

Another major factor in understanding the rhetoric–reality gap is an examination of the language used. There is considerable confusion in this area across all dimensions of parental involvement. The issue of what is really being said is itself filled with contradictions and anomalies. Although there is, on one level, a consensus that parental involvement is desirable and worthwhile, there remains throughout the literature an array of theories and ideas concerning the "how" and "what" of that involvement. The language that is used to describe both the participants and the processes involved defines the interactions to some extent. For example, when talking about "parents and professionals," the language itself defines one, professionals, as experts and the others, parents, as nonexperts (Bastiani, 1993; Munn, 1993; Wolfendale, 1983).

In addition, a widespread use of the term "partnership" has been developed at all levels from school brochures to government policy papers. Despite its wonderful "feel-good" nature, its use is problematic. The use of language such as partnership, collaboration, and participation masks the inequalities that exist in reality in the practice of parental involvement (Reay, 1998; Wolfendale, 1983). Despite the use of terms such as partnership, which, according to Bastiani (1993), should actually be about shared purpose, negotiation, and mutual respect, home–school relationships are typically much more adversarial, and about rights and power. According to Bastiani (1989), parents' experience is often of a system that "talks with a forked tongue" (p. 8). Similarly, Hegarty (1993, p. 129) describes the word "partnership" as filling people with a "warm glow of right thinking," but criticizes it because it leads to feelings of complacency that are counterproductive to action. He argues that it is a term that has vastly different meanings to different people and that, although often used with little recourse to its implications in terms of power or practice, it is in reality about a process.

Drawing on the literature, Lueder (2000) provides an interesting example of the imbalance between the language used and the underlying meaning and intent.

Lueder discusses the gap between rhetoric and reality and talks of the need to shift our thinking to schools working with and supporting families. He bases his model of parent–school interactions on the theory that there is a central problem in parental support of education because large numbers of parents, whom he names "missing parents," are not involved in education at home. He proposes a "self-renewing partnership model" of parental involvement based on the idea of what he terms "energy-in," which is an extension of the traditional roles of families in supporting schools, and "energy-out," which involves schools supporting families. He presents a detailed list comprising eight "Parent Partner Roles," which are ways by which parents can support the school. The list is hierarchical with each step depending upon the prior one and viewing parents through such roles as nurturer, communicator, supporter, advisor, and collaborator. There is recognition of the barriers that many families face, which he categorizes as either family, school, or community-based barriers. In recognizing that some parents may be disenfranchised from school, he has formulated a "Strategic Partnership Planning System" to help identify "family populations to be targeted," and to select strategies and best practices to help them resolve their problems (Lueder, p. 6).

Lueder's work contains considerable sound and well supported theory and the language he uses leaves the reader thinking that this is indeed a book about parental partnership. However, critically analyzing the substance of his model illustrates the problem that exists so often with the language used. Though the model focuses on "partnership" as its overall aim, the reality is that the model may be counterproductive to building a real partnership since it appears to assume that parents are problems (see Chap. 1). The model is based on the principle that parents are "failing" and need help from experts to ensure that education operates as it should and that the, "case of the missing parents can be solved" (Lueder, 2000, p. 7). A partnership based on the premise that one party is a problem is likely to be doomed from the start. It is parental understanding of this covert agenda that inhibits the success of many such plans to increase parental involvement.

Further, although the term "parent partner roles" creates that "warm glow of right thinking" that Hegarty (1993, p. 129) referred to, the content of each of Lueder's (2000) eight steps is concerned only with school directives of how parents should engage with schools. As a partnership it is one-sided, presenting no accommodation to, or even acknowledgment of, parents' goals, but instead aiming to employ parents in such a way that school agendas and concerns are met. This is at odds with the notion of partnership suggested by Bastiani (1993) where there is mutual respect and shared purpose. In fact, the stated purpose of the energy-out half of the model, where the language so nicely refers to schools reaching out to support families, is "to create the collaborative relationships and to enhance the families' willingness and ability to play their Parent Partner Roles" (Lueder, p. 6). In this respect, the model appears to be simply a tool for schools to groom and shape parents to ensure that they meet goals that the "experts" have developed. This illustrates the fact that there is a gap between rhetoric and reality in part because the language of the rhetoric itself is not in harmony with the substance of that rhetoric.

Societal Factors

Historical and Demographic Factors

Further understanding of the development of the rhetoric–reality gap can be found in examining the historical context in which parental involvement occurs. Behind the gap lies an historical background of social and educational development (Bastiani, 1989). The history involved provides an often unacknowledged barrier to involving parents in education. For example, Henderson and Berla (1994) point out that school organization, historically structured along factory production lines, continues today. This is a largely accepted part of our school culture that is an obstacle for both teachers and parents in their efforts to collaborate more. Many schools still bear the hallmarks of the formality and inflexibility that characterized schooling historically, and which are counterproductive to forming parent–school relationships that require flexibility.

Also, traditional definitions of parental involvement have been narrow, with a central focus on supporting the school and fund-raising within an environment where schools assumed responsibility for and power over the education provided. Although modern times have seen a major shift, with parents now being seen as having an important role to play in education, many attitudes and perceptions that have their roots in this traditional heritage continue to linger. Generally, governments are supportive of the devolution of power to parents, partly since it suits other agendas they have, but it has come at a time when there are also major changes to family structures, mobility, and work, which are all in opposition to improved parental involvement (OECD, 1997).

These changing family structures are marked by an increase in parental working hours and mobility, greater numbers of families in which both parents work, accompanied by an increased number of divorces, resulting in increases in sole parenting and the number of repartnered families. Concurrently, there are fewer extended family arrangements, a decrease in religious practice, and increased community fragmentation, as well as greater individualism and competition (David, Edwards, Hughes & Ribbens, 1993; OECD, 1997). The combined effect of these factors is that significant numbers of parents are operating with higher stress levels, less money, and less time, which makes it difficult to develop optimal involvement in the education of their children.

Political Factors

At government level, several factors act as barriers to parental involvement. There is an absence of specific legislation on parental involvement, so it is not surprising that espoused policy on such involvement, which relies on voluntary participation by schools, leads to uneven practice (Macbeth, 1984). Inconsistency within different sections of education legislation and differences between government policy and action also play roles in limiting the practice of parental involvement. For example, governments may outwardly support parental involvement yet concurrently undermine it through other policies that are in conflict with this support (Bastiani, 1993; Munn, 1993). This can be seen in New Zealand and the UK where governments simultaneously seek to promote parental involvement through initiatives such as the "Schooling Strategy" (MoE, 2005) in New Zealand and the "Children's Plan" (DCSF, 2007) in the UK, while at the same time pursuing the politics of educational consumerism that pushes parents and schools toward competition rather than cooperation. Further, unless government policy on parental involvement is accompanied by appropriate action, such as strategic implementation, information dissemination, and training, it is unlikely to be effective in improving parental involvement. Government failure in these areas results in a lack of consistency in approach, the implementation of policy being fragmented and therefore barriers to parental involvement remaining in place.

One determiner of the levels of parental involvement that is decided at a political level is the way school systems are organized. For example, New Zealand schools have catchment zones, which mean that the vast majority of children attending them live in the community in which the school is located. Where school zones do not operate, as in most parts of the UK, many of the children attending live outside the community in which the school is based, which makes it more difficult for schools to build partnerships with parents (Epstein, 2001).

Another example of how decisions at national government level affect parental involvement is in the issue of teacher training. The content of teacher education programs in countries such as New Zealand and the UK has in recent years been largely set by government education policies. Yet, despite the policies promoting parental involvement noted above (DCSF, 2007; MoE, 2005), there is still no requirement to include courses on working with parents and families in teacher education programs. The importance of such courses for providing teachers with the skills to work effectively with parents has been widely acknowledged (Epstein, 2001; Greenwood & Hickman, 1991), but because government policies do not require these, they are typically not included. This is in contrast with the situation in the USA where accreditation standards (National Council for Accreditation of Teacher Education, 2002) require the topic of parental involvement to be a compulsory course in teacher education programs. However, a recent survey of the staff who teach these courses has concluded that they do not include sufficient practical experiences of parental involvement to ensure that teachers are adequately prepared to work effectively with parents (Flanigan, 2007).

Economic Factors

Closely aligned with these political issues are factors of economics and funding. In many Western countries, free market policies have come to dominate economics, resulting in education being organized to service the needs of the market. In essence, education practices have to justify their share of available funding while operating in a field that is continually evaluated for increased performance by such means as national tests of literacy and numeracy. Programs aimed at increasing parental involvement are disadvantaged in this climate because they are concerned with a process relating to long-term rather than short-term goals (Bastiani, 1993). The result of these conflicting pressures between the educational market and funding is that there is little or no money assigned to develop parental involvement, which clearly limits programs, resources, training, and further research (Adelman, 1992; Sanders, 2006). The impact of the market on the reality of parental involvement is such that economic constraints are echoed in the constraints on such involvement (Hegarty, 1993).

An example of this is the "Home–School Liaison Scheme," which was set up by Humberside Local Education Authority in England in 1988. In this scheme, schools in deprived areas in and around Hull were provided with additional funding so they could employ Home–School Liaison Teachers (HSLT) who worked half-time in this role and half-time as classroom teachers. The 43 HSLTs appointed received additional training focused on developing effective parental involvement in their schools. The HSLT role focused on developing partnerships between parents and schools, which included setting up parent rooms, providing parent education, and relieving class teachers so that they could make home visits. Despite the clear benefits to schools that resulted from this scheme, when finances for Local Education Authorities were reduced by central government in the 1990s, the HSLT scheme was one of the first services to be cut.

Summary and Conclusion

The issue of parental involvement in education is notable for the extensive rhetoric supporting it and considerable variation in the reality of its practice. Clarification of the specific factors responsible for the rhetoric–reality gap is considered a necessary precursor to the further development of the practice of parental involvement in education. The explanatory model presented in this chapter is intended to help all those concerned with the education of children gain a greater understanding of these factors and thereby encourage more widespread development of effective practice with regard to parental involvement. The model has also been developed so that it can be used in the preservice and in-service training of school and educational psychologists, counselors, social workers, teachers, and other professionals who work in the education system. Studying the explanatory model will enable these professionals to gain greater insight into the factors that act as barriers to, and facilitate the development of, effective parental involvement. This will enable such professionals to develop more effective practices with regard to parental involvement in education so that they can optimize the impact of this important aspect of the educational process.

Through studying the explanatory model described in this chapter, it is evident that the issue of parental involvement in education is a complex matter that requires educators to move beyond simplistic notions about the underlying factors that affect the effectiveness of parental involvement. The barriers to effective parental involvement discussed in this chapter provide an explanation for the existence of the gap between rhetoric and reality with regard to such involvement. Collecting the various factors together in the model presented has made it clear that parental involvement is shaped and limited by a divergent range of barriers related to parents and families, children, parent–teacher differences, and societal issues.

The model is also intended to be used to generate ideas for further research on parental involvement. Some aspects of the model have been well researched, such as the demographic factors that influence the involvement of parents, but little research has been conducted on others, such as differences between parents and teachers in their perceptions of and goals for parental involvement. Another aspect of involvement on which there has been little research to date is the actual policies and practices of parental involvement used in schools. This is the focus of the next three chapters.

Chapter 3
Model for Parental Involvement in

Introduction

In the literature on parental involvement, various approaches to parent–professional relationships can be identified, each defined by a different set of assumptions, goals, and strategies. These approaches range from those that attempt to minimize parental involvement to others that actively promote it. The approaches can be conceptualized in the form of models for the practice of parental involvement. The six most common models, the protective, expert, transmission, curriculum enrichment, consumer, and partnership models are described below.

Protective Model

In the protective model, the main aim is to avoid conflict by separating professional and parenting functions. For example, the teacher's role is to educate children at school, whereas the parent's role is to make sure children get to school on time with the correct equipment. Parental involvement in schools is seen as an unnecessary and potentially damaging interference in the efficient education of children. Swap (1993) considers that this approach is the most common model of parent–teacher relationships.

Expert Model

In the expert model (Cunningham & Davis, 1985), professionals regard themselves as experts on all aspects of the development and education of children, while parents' views are accorded little credence. In this model, professionals maintain control over educational decisions, while the parent's role is to receive information and instructions about their children. A major problem with this approach is that it encourages parents to be submissive and dependent on professionals. Parents are

G. Hornby, *Parental Involvement in Childhood Education: Building Effective School-Family Partnerships*, DOI 10.1007/978-1-4419-8379-4_3,
© Springer Science+Business Media, LLC 2011

to question professionals' decisions and tend to lose faith in their own
tence. Another problem is that since professionals do not make use of the rich
rce of knowledge parents have about their children, they tend to overlook important problems or abilities that the children have. In addition, professionals working
within the expert model will not be aware of any difficulties that parents themselves
might experience. All these factors increase the possibility that parents will be dissa-
tisfied with the service they get from professionals who adopt this approach.

Transmission Model

In the transmission model (Swap, 1993), parents' help is enlisted to support the
goals of the school. The model is employed by professionals who regard themselves as the main sources of expertise on children but who recognize the benefits
of using parents as a resource. They consider that some of their expertise can be
transmitted to parents so that parents can carry out some form of intervention with
their children. A well-known example of this approach in the field of education is
a paired reading program in which parents are trained to help their children with
reading at home (Topping, 1986).

In this model, the professional remains in control and decides on the interventions to be used but does accept that parents can play an important part in facilitating
their children's progress. Therefore, there is more likelihood that parents' views
will be considered and their concerns addressed. However, in order to use this
approach, professionals need additional skills such as techniques for effectively
guiding parents and the interpersonal skills required for establishing productive
working relationships with them. These factors will increase the likelihood of parents'
being satisfied with the service they receive and reduce the tendency for them to
become dependent on professionals.

The danger of this approach is the assumption that all parents can and should
take on the role of acting as a resource. This risks overburdening some parents by
placing excessive demands on them to carry out intervention programs with their
children. The chances of this happening are increased for children with special
educational needs (SEN) since several different professionals, such as speech therapists,
psychologists, and teachers may all be expecting parents to carry out intervention
programs at home.

Curriculum-Enrichment Model

The goal of the curriculum-enrichment model (Swap, 1993) is to extend the school
curriculum by incorporating parents' contributions. It is based on the assumption
that parents have important expertise to contribute and that the interaction between
parents and teachers around the implementation of the curriculum material will
enhance the educational objectives of the school. The focus of parental involvement in
this model is mainly on curriculum and instruction within schools. An example of an

area of the curriculum for which this approach has been widely used is multicultural education. Parents from various ethnic, religious, and cultural groups have been able to collaborate with teachers to develop and implement curricula that accurately reflect the history, values, and views of the groups that they represent.

This model suggests a novel way of involving parents in children's learning that increases the resources available to the school and provides opportunities for parents and teachers to learn from each other. Its major drawback is that to implement this model it requires that schools allow parents to have a major input in what is taught and how it is taught, which can be threatening to many teachers.

Consumer Model

In the consumer model (Cunningham & Davis, 1985), parents are regarded as being consumers of educational services. The professional acts as a consultant, while the parent decides what action is to be taken. The parent has control over the decision-making process, while the professional's role is to provide them with relevant information and a range of options from which to choose. Thus, in this approach, the professional defers to parents, who are effectively placed in the expert role. The professional's role is to listen to parents' views and help them choose from the alternatives available. As parents are in control of the decision-making process in this approach, they are likely to be much more satisfied with the service they receive, feel more competent about their parenting, and are also less likely to become dependent on professionals.

The danger of this approach is that, taken to its extreme, it can lead to an abdication of professional responsibility, which I observed while working as an educational psychologist, when a colleague adopted an extreme form of the consumer model. This psychologist would handle the selection of an appropriate educational placement for a child by simply showing parents around a variety of schools and getting them to choose one. Without the benefit of professional guidance, parents were encouraged to make uninformed decisions that may not have been in their children's best interests. In this way, parents were placed in the role of experts on how their children's educational needs could be met, which is just as inappropriate as professionals regarding themselves as experts on all aspects of children's functioning and adopting the expert model in their relationships with parents.

Partnership Model

The most appropriate model for relationships between professionals working in education and parents is considered to be the partnership model. This is one in which professionals are viewed as experts on education and parents are viewed as experts on their children. The relationship between professionals and parents can then be a partnership that involves the sharing of expertise and control to provide the optimum education for children. Parents and professionals can contribute different strengths to their relationship, thereby increasing the potency of the partnership. For example, most parents have strong emotional attachments to their children and, therefore, make excellent advocates for them. However, the emotional attachment also tends to make them somewhat subjective when considering their children's abilities and needs, which is why the objectivity that professionals bring to the partnership is so important.

According to Turnbull et al. (2011) there are seven principles of effective partnerships between professionals, such as psychologists or teachers, and parents. These are discussed below.

Trust

The key principle of effective partnerships is building trust in relationships. This involves professionals being reliable, maintaining confidentiality, using sound judgment, plus being open and honest in all dealings with parents.

Respect

An essential aspect of effective partnership is that it is based on mutual respect. For example, it requires parents and professionals to listen to each other and give due consideration to each other's views. This involves treating others with dignity, affirming strengths, and respecting cultural diversity.

Competence

In order for partnerships to work, parents must have confidence in the competence of professionals. For teachers, this means providing a quality education, setting high expectations for children, and continuing to develop new knowledge and skills. Competent teachers will develop a range of opportunities for parents to be involved to promote children's learning both at school and at home.

Communication

Effective partnerships require two-way communication between parents and professionals. This involves both partners listening to each other so that, for example, parents can share information on their children's needs and teachers can provide information about children's progress at school. This requires professionals to be friendly, to listen well, and to be able to provide information clearly and sensitively.

Commitment

Effective partnership also requires a long-term commitment to a wide range of activities involving both professionals and parents. It involves ensuring availability and accessibility, being sensitive to emotional needs, and going above and beyond expectations when necessary.

Equality

Professionals and parents need to be involved in joint problem solving, planning, and decision making, which for teachers may be at the levels of individual children, the classroom, and the school. Professionals and parents must support one another's efforts, for example, teachers can provide guidance on how parents can help children at home and parents can act as voluntary helpers at school. This involves professionals sharing power, fostering the empowerment of parents, and providing options for children.

Advocacy

Effective partnerships involve identifying problems early, preventing problems from developing, creating win-win solutions, and being alert for opportunities to advocate for children.

When these principles of partnership are developed, effective collaborative working relationships between professionals and parents can be established. However, having the partnership model as an overall guide does not preclude the use of interventions based on the other approaches when they would be more appropriate. For example, the transmission model appropriately provides the underlying rationale for many parent involvement projects, such as home–school reading schemes. Also, the adoption of the expert model is justified in prescribing treatment, such a personal therapy or parenting skills programs, for parents who have subjected their children to physical, emotional, or sexual abuse (Morgan, 1985).

In fact, some interventions, such as parent education programs, can be organized from different perspectives depending on the group of parents to be involved. That is, they can be organized from the perspective of the consumer model with parents stipulating what guidance or input they would like. Alternatively, they can be organized from the perspective of the expert model with teachers specifying what parents need to learn. For example, parents of children with special needs may be able and willing to select suitable input (consumer model), whereas parents who have subjected their children to some form of abuse are likely to need professionals to decide what input would be most beneficial (expert).

Therefore, although there must be enough flexibility to enable other models to be used when necessary, it is considered that the partnership model is generally the most appropriate perspective from which to develop constructive parental involvement. In this model, professionals are aware of addressing parents' needs and of acknowledging the various ways parents can contribute to the development and education of their children. This will facilitate the development of effective partnerships between parents and professionals. In order for such partnerships to become more than just lofty ideals, the concept needs to be developed into a model for parent involvement that is designed to guide practice. This is considered in the next section.

The Need for a Model for Parental Involvement

The evolution of parental involvement in education over the past 40 years has tended to be practice-led rather than being guided by theory or policy. Many examples of interesting parental involvement projects are in existence around the world, and useful models are available for various types of parental involvement. Also, numerous books have been written with the intention of providing professionals with the knowledge necessary to build effective relationship with parents (e.g., Atkin, Bastiani, & Goode, 1988; Bastiani, 1987, 1988, 1989; Berger, 1991; Epstein 2001; Featherstone, 1981; Grant & Ray, 2010; Hornby, 1995, 2000; Kroth, 1985; Lombana, 1983; McConkey, 1985; Seligman, 2000; Simpson, 1996; Topping, 1986; Turnbull, Turnbull, Erwin, Soodak, & Shogren, 2011; Wolfendale, 1983, 1989, 1992).

However, none of these books has focused specifically on what activities schools typically use and therefore what teachers can do to improve the practice of parental involvement in their schools, which is the central theme of this book. As a first step toward this goal, it is necessary to develop a vision of what effective parental involvement would look like. The best way to do this was considered to be to produce a comprehensive theoretical model for parental involvement. Such a model can then be used to provide professionals working in schools, such as psychologists and teachers, with a framework with which to formulate overall policy and plans for working with parents. The model also enables each school to conduct an audit of its current practice of parental involvement to ensure that, as far as possible, parents needs are being met and their potential contributions are being utilized.

Model for Parent Involvement

The theoretical model for parental involvement described below was developed by combining and adapting existing models (e.g., Bastiani, 1989; Epstein 2000; Kroth, 1985; Lombana, 1983; Wolfendale, 1992) and by gaining feedback from numerous groups of parents, teachers, and other professionals who work in schools. The model was originally devised with teachers and parents of children with SEN in mind (Hornby, 1989), but it was subsequently realized that, with slight adaptations, it was equally applicable to all parents and teachers (Hornby, 1990). The model for parental involvement that was developed and has been used by the author for the past 20 years in teacher education and professional development courses is presented in Fig. 3.1.

The model consists of two pyramids connected at the base, one representing a hierarchy of parents' needs, the other a hierarchy of parents' strengths or possible contributions. Both pyramids demonstrate visually the different levels of needs and contributions of parents. Thus, while all parents have some needs and some potential contributions that can be utilized, a smaller number have an intense need for guidance, or the capability of making an extensive contribution.

PARENTAL CONTRIBUTIONS

SOME   **POLICY FORMATION**

e.g. PTA members, school governors,
parent support/advocay groups

MANY   **ACTING AS A RESOURCE**

e.g. classroom aides, fund-raising,
supporting other parents

MOST   **COLLABORATING WITH TEACHERS**

e.g. home-school reading, maths
and behavior programs

ALL   **SHARING INFORMATION ON CHILDREN**

e.g. children's strengths, weaknesses,
likes, dislikes, medical details

ALL   **CHANNELS OF COMMUNICATION**

e.g. handbooks, newsletters, telephone
contacts, homework diaries

MOST   **LIAISON WITH SCHOOL STAFF**

e.g. home visits, parent-teacher meetings

MANY   **PARENT EDUCATION**

e.g. parent workshops

SOME   **PARENT SUPPORT**

e.g. counselling, support groups

PARENTAL NEEDS

Fig. 3.1 Model for parental involvement

Each of the components of the model are outlined and the knowledge and skills needed by teachers to participate in each type of parental involvement are identified.

Parental Contributions

Policy Formation

Some parents are able to contribute their expertise through membership of parent or professional organizations. This includes being a school governor, a member of the Parent–Teacher Association (PTA), or being involved in a parent support or advocacy group. Others have the time and ability to provide in-service training for professionals by speaking at conferences or workshops, or by writing about their experiences (e.g., Featherstone, 1981). Teachers should continually be on the lookout for parents who can contribute in this way so that their abilities can be used to the full.

Acting as a Resource

Many parents have the time and ability to act as voluntary teacher aides, either assisting in the classroom or in the preparation of materials or in fund-raising. Others may have special skills that they can contribute, such as helping prepare newsletters, in craft activities, or in curriculum areas in which they have a special talent. Some parents may have the time, skills, and knowledge to provide support to other parents either informally or perhaps through participation in self-help or support groups. During these times of contracting professional resources, teachers should make sure that they make optimum use of this valuable voluntary resource. It is often the case that parents also benefit from acting as a resource. They may acquire knowledge that is helpful to their understanding of their own children. In addition, they are often observed to gain in confidence through helping at school and go on to further their own education. In order to enable as many parents as possible to act as a resource to the school, teachers need good communication skills (see Chap. 7).

Collaborating with Teachers

Most parents are willing and able to contribute more than just information. Most parents are able to collaborate with teachers by reinforcing classroom programs at home, such as in home–school reading programs (Topping, 1986). However, some parents, at times, are not able to carry out work at home with their children. This can be very frustrating for teachers, since they realize that collaboration between home and school results in children making greater progress, so children whose parents do not work closely with them are likely to develop more slowly. However, teachers have to accept that some parents at some point in time are simply not able to collaborate in this way. It is probably because their resources are already fully committed in coping with their children at home, so they are not able to do anything extra.

At a later time, family circumstances may change and parents may then be able to become more involved in their children's education. Teachers must respect parents' rights to make this decision in consideration of the wider needs of their families. So, while involvement in home–school programs, or other requests for parents to carry out work with their children at home, should always be offered to all parents, including those who have not collaborated in the past, it should be expected that a small proportion of parents will not participate. Therefore, teachers need the skills of collaborating with parents in a flexible partnership in which parents' choices are respected.

Sharing Information on Children

All parents can contribute valuable information about their children because they have known them throughout their lives and have been the ones who have participated in all previous contacts with professionals to assess and plan for meeting their children's needs. Information concerning children's likes and dislikes, strengths and weaknesses, along with any relevant medical details, can be gathered by teachers at parent–teacher meetings. Making full use of parents' knowledge of their children not only leads to more effective professional practice, but it also makes parents feel that they have been listened to and that an active interest has been taken in their children. Therefore, teachers need to develop good listening and interviewing skills (Atkin et al., 1988; Seligman, 2000).

Parental Needs

Channels of Communication

All parents need to have effective channels of communication with their children's teachers. They need information about the organization and requirements of the school as it affects their child. They need to know when their children are having difficulties and what the school is going to do to address these. Also, parents need to know about their rights and responsibilities. This can be provided through handbooks or regular newsletters written especially for parents.

Parents need to feel that they can contact the school at any time when they have a concern about their child. Some parents prefer to communicate by telephone, others would rather call in to see the teacher face-to-face, while still others find that contact through written notes or home–school diaries suits them best. Therefore, educators need to develop effective written and oral communication skills and ensure that a wide range of communication options are open to parents. However, the most important factor in maintaining good communication is the openness to parents that schools demonstrate through their contacts with parents. The attitude of choice has often been referred to as an "open door policy" in which parents feel comfortable about contacting or going into the school when they have a concern (Bastiani 1987).

Liaison with School Staff

Most parents want to know how their children are getting on at school. They want to find out what their children have achieved and whether they are having any difficulties. They regard teachers as the main source of information on their children's performance at school and therefore need to have a working partnership with them. Teachers can facilitate this by keeping in regular contact with parents through such means as telephone calls, home visits, home–school notebooks, weekly report cards and by meeting with parents at school. These strategies are discussed in detail in Chap. 6.

Teachers are often disappointed that some parents do not come to parent–teacher meetings at school, thereby giving the impression that they are not interested in how their children are progressing. However, there are usually other reasons for them not turning up, such as the difficulties involved in getting a babysitter, the overwhelming demands of looking after their family, or anxieties about coming to school related to the negative experiences they themselves had at school. It is important then for teachers to find other ways of liaising with these parents, perhaps by having regular telephone contacts or home visits. Therefore, teachers need to develop the skills of conducting formal and informal meetings with parents. In addition, they need to offer a range of options for liaison with parents so that those who do not feel comfortable coming to formal meetings with teachers have other forms of regular contact made available to them (Simpson, 1996).

Parent Education

Many parents are interested in participating in parent education programs aimed at promoting their children's progress or managing their behavior. Parent education can be conducted individually or in parent groups or workshops (Topping, 1986). Some parents will not want to take part in such programs, for a variety of reasons. There will be those who, at a certain point in time, feel confident about the way they are parenting their children and do not see the need for parent education. Later, when their children reach a different developmental stage, they may think differently. For other parents, there will be practical difficulties such as arranging babysitters or transport. However, a substantial number of parents are interested in being involved in parent education workshops, and most of those who do participate get a tremendous amount out of it. Ideally then, opportunities for group parent education should be made available to all parents.

It seems that the most effective format for parent education is one that combines guidance about promoting children's development with opportunities for parents to discuss their concerns (Pugh & De'Ath, 1984). Parent education programs that involve a group of parents, and employ a workshop format, easily lend themselves to providing a combination of educational input and sharing of concerns. This type of format enables parents to learn new skills and gain confidence through talking to other parents and teachers (Hornby & Murray, 1983). To be involved in parent education, therefore, teachers need to have the listening and counseling skills discussed in Chap. 7.

Parent Support

Some parents, at times, are in need of supportive counseling, even though they may not actually request it. This support can be provided either individually or in group counseling sessions. Although such support should be available to all parents, the majority of parents seldom need extensive counseling. The fact is that if parents have good channels of communication and regular liaison with teachers, coupled with the opportunity to receive guidance about their children whenever they need it, then only a few of them will need counseling at any particular time. Whereas most parents are reluctant to seek the help of professional counselors, they will approach their children's teachers in search of guidance or counseling for the problems that concern them. Teachers should, therefore, have a level of basic counseling skills sufficient to be good listeners and to help parents solve everyday problems. They should also have the knowledge necessary to be able to refer parents to professional counselors when problems raised are beyond their level of competence (Hornby, Hall & Hall, 2003).

Using the Model to Investigate Parent Involvement Practices

The model has been used to generate a checklist of questions designed to investigate whether school policies and procedures are in place to meet parents' needs and that parents' potential contributions are being fully utilized. The checklist provides examples of the kinds of questions that need to be asked when reviewing a school's policy and practices regarding parental involvement. Each element of the model for parental involvement is considered in turn and questions to be posed are suggested.

The checklist was used as an interview schedule to survey the policies and practices of parental involvement in elementary, middle, and secondary schools, the findings of which are reported in Chaps. 4 and 5. The checklist was supplemented by adding three related topics at the end of the interview schedule, "Encouraging Parents into School," "Diverse Parents" and "Professional development" to gain additional information on parental involvement policies and practices in schools. The interview schedule generated from the model for parental involvement is presented below.

Parent Involvement Interview Schedule

Policy Formation

- *Does the school have a separate written policy on parent involvement?* Does the policy clearly specify parents' rights and responsibilities and is it included in material distributed to all parents and teachers?

- *Have parents been involved in the formulation of this policy?* For example, have the PTA or parents on the Board of Trustees (BoT) had input into the policy design process?
- *What monitoring procedures are in place to ensure that the policy is implemented?* For example, how is feedback obtained from parents?
- *Is there an active PTA or equivalent at the school?* What proportion of parents participate in PTA activities?
- *How are parents' views sought about school policies or procedures?* For example, are questionnaire surveys used?
- *Is there a room set aside for parents' use?* Do parents use a spare classroom, or can the staffroom be used by parents during lesson times?
- *What means are there for encouraging parents to become members of the PTA or BoT?* Who identifies parents that could contribute to the school in capacities such as membership of the PTA or BoT?

Acting as a Resource

- *In what kinds of activities does the school welcome help from parents?* Are parents used to listen to children read or to assist in teaching or in preparing classroom materials?
- *Who is responsible for ensuring that parents with a particular talent for leadership are identified and encouraged to put their abilities to use?* Do all teachers know they can do this?
- *How are parents informed about the ways in which they can help at the school?* For example, is there a parents' handbook or a regular newsletter?
- *How is voluntary help from parents organized within the school?* For example, is a particular member of staff assigned to coordinate the help or is it seen as the responsibility of each teacher?

Collaborating with Teachers

- *How are the results of school assessments communicated to parents?* Are individual parent–teacher meetings held and if so, how often?
- *How do parents contribute to the assessment of their child's needs?* For example, by being asked for their observations or by completing proformas or developmental checklists.
- *What input do parents have in deciding the goals and teaching priorities for their children?* For example, do parents discuss with teachers the emphasis which should be placed on developing academic skills or social skills, as part of personal and social education curricula.

- *How are parents encouraged to reinforce school programs at home?* For example, are they expected to participate in a paired reading scheme?
- *Are parents given a choice about the level of their involvement at home with their children?* Is there discussion with parents beforehand so that they are not pressured into participating in projects that they cannot afford the time or energy to carry out?

Sharing Information on Children

- *How is information on children's special needs, medical conditions, and relevant family circumstances gathered from parents?* For example, through home visits, parent–teacher meetings, or contacts with previous schools?
- *How is relevant information from parents disseminated to all members of staff who work with their children?* What systems are used to record, and communicate to teachers, information about such things as children's special needs and the medication they require?
- *What use is made of parents' insights on their children?* For example, parents' knowledge of their children's strengths and weaknesses, likes and dislikes, or how they respond to different approaches.

Channels of Communication

- *How does the school pass on information to parents about their rights and responsibilities and about school organization?* For example, is this information sent out in handbooks specifically aimed at parents or by holding meetings at which school policies are discussed?
- *Does the school have balanced procedures for contacting parents?* That is, are parents contacted to inform them of their children's achievements as well as their difficulties, or are they only contacted when there is a problem?
- *Does a member of staff visit families before pupils start to attend the school?* Are home visits scheduled when children are changing schools, moving from primary to secondary school, or being reintegrated following a period in a special school?
- *What guidelines are available for parents on visiting the school to talk over a concern with their children's teachers?* For example, do they have to go through the principal, make an appointment directly with the teacher, or just come in whenever they can.
- *What channels of communication are there between parents and teachers?* That is, can parents choose to phone, write notes to teachers, make an appointment to see teachers, or drop in to the school when necessary?

Liaison with school Staff

- *What are the frequency and purpose of parent–teacher meetings?* For example, are parents invited to attend termly or yearly meetings to review their children's progress?
- *Do parents regularly receive home visits?* Are home visits made at least once a year, or only when there is a problem? Are visits made by class teachers or senior members of staff? Is there flexibility in the time of day used so that both parents can be present?
- *What kinds of formal reports are sent home and how often?* Are reports sent home termly or yearly?
- *Are home–school diaries used with some children?* For example, are they used for children with SEN or for those with behavioral difficulties? Are the diaries used daily or weekly?

Parent Education

- *Are parents invited into the school to observe teaching in progress?* For example, are they invited to observe either their own child or other children in the school?
- *When are teachers available to provide guidance to parents?* Do teachers make home visits in order to provide guidance to parents or does this only occur in parent–teacher meetings at school?
- *Are parent workshops organized by the school?* For example, are there workshops for parents of children with reading difficulties or behavior problems?
- *Are parents informed about opportunities for parent education in the community?* How is information about parenting courses made available to parents?

Parent Support

- *How are parents given opportunities to discuss their concerns on a one-to-one basis?* For example, is this done on home visits or specially scheduled parent–teacher meetings at school?
- *Are opportunities provided for parents to share their concerns with other parents?* For example, are parents introduced to other parents of children with similar difficulties or given opportunity of attending parent workshops?
- *Do teachers know where to refer parents for supportive counseling?* Is there an awareness of services and groups within the local community that can provide supportive counseling such as social workers or self-help groups?
- *Are parents encouraged to participate in support groups and parent organizations outside the school?* For example, Parent-to-Parent services.

Encouraging Parents into School

- *What activities are used to ensure that all parents establish contact with the school?*
- Open days/nights
- New parents' evenings
- School performances
- Talks by well known invited speakers
- Exhibitions of work by the pupils
- School fairs
- School/class barbeques
- Others
- *What is done to overcome barriers to parent involvement?* That is, to make all parents feel more comfortable about coming in to school

Involving Diverse Parents

- *What adaptations does the school use to work effectively with diverse parents?* That is, those with children with SEN or gifted children, as well as those parents from different ethnic groups and/or language backgrounds
- *How are parents of children with special needs involved in developing their child's Individual Educational Plan?* For example, do they attend all the meetings and have a chance to discuss their child with any outside specialists involved?
- *How are parents of gifted children involved in planning extension programs for them?* For example, are parent–teacher meetings used for this?
- *How is parental involvement in reviews of their children's progress optimized?* For example, by obtaining their observations in writing beforehand and being active members of the review team
- *What is done to work effectively with parents from different cultures or those whose main language is not English?* For example, how are translators and interpreters used?

Professional Development for Teachers

- *What training do teachers get on how to work effectively with parents?* Is this done in preservice or in-service courses?
- *Are parents involved in professional development sessions with teachers?* For example, have parents of children with SEN or gifted children been invited to talk about their experiences, expectations, needs, and possible contributions?

Summary and Conclusion

This chapter presents a review of professional approaches to working with parents based on various models. This helps to clarify the form of parent–teacher relationship that is considered to be the most productive, which is a partnership model. It is suggested that a theoretical model for parental involvement is needed to assist schools to design policies and procedures for involving parents. The model proposed addresses parents' needs and their potential contributions and suggests competencies needed by teachers to ensure its successful implementation. The model is also used to generate a checklist of questions that schools can employ to evaluate their practice of parental involvement in order to identify strengths and areas that need further development. The checklist, with some additional questions, was used as an interview schedule to survey the policies and practices of parental involvement in elementary, middle, and secondary schools. The findings of these surveys are reported in Chaps. 4 and 5.

Chapter 4
Parent Involvement in Elementary Schools

Introduction

An extensive international literature now supports the potential of parental involvement for improving children's academic achievements and social outcomes. This research also suggests that naturally occurring parental involvement in schools is generally more effective than externally initiated home–school programs (Pomerantz, Moorman, & Litwack, 2007). It is therefore important to investigate parental involvement practices in schools so that guidance on effective involvement can be based on actual evidence from schools. The focus of this chapter is on the findings of surveys of parental involvement practices in elementary schools in New Zealand, as well as case studies of parental involvement practices in elementary schools in England and Barbados.

Research on parental involvement in New Zealand has so far only been published in the form of local reports and students' theses. The findings of much of this New Zealand research, and that of selected international literature related to parental involvement, have been summarized in a major report commissioned by the New Zealand Ministry of Education (Biddulph, Biddulph, & Biddulph, 2003). This influential report is often referred to in the New Zealand educational literature as the source of the finding that effective partnerships between parents and schools result in improved outcomes for children.

Following on from this report, there have been two further reviews of research and practices of parental involvement in New Zealand. One was a study of partnerships between parents and schools, conducted as part of regular reviews (inspections) of schools (Education Review Office, 2008). Evidence was gathered from 233 schools, including elementary, middle, and secondary schools. An analysis of the reviews found that recommendations were made to nearly three quarters of the schools to improve engagement with parents. It was also recommended that the majority of schools needed to improve some aspects of their parental involvement practices. The other study, which focused on home–school partnerships, drew evidence from seven New Zealand and seven international case studies, as well as four evaluations of home–school initiatives in New Zealand (Bull,

G. Hornby, *Parental Involvement in Childhood Education: Building Effective School-Family Partnerships*, DOI 10.1007/978-1-4419-8379-4_4,
© Springer Science+Business Media, LLC 2011

Brooking, & Campbell, 2008). It concluded that there was little empirical support
for the benefits of home–school initiatives, in contrast to the extensive literature
supporting the beneficial effects of "naturally occurring or spontaneous parental
involvement in education" (p. 57).

This differential impact of specific forms of provision for parental involvement
is supported by the recent synthesis of international research on educational interventions, conducted by a New Zealand academic (Hattie, 2009), which reported a
low effect size of 0.16 for home–school programs but an above average effect size
of 0.51 for overall parental involvement. This difference is also supported by findings
from the international literature (Pomerantz et al., 2007), which reports that the
naturally occurring parental involvement in schools is more effective than externally initiated home–school programs, such as those reviewed by Bull et al. (2008)
that was referred to above.

Given the findings of the international literature and the three recent New
Zealand reports, it was considered timely to investigate what parental involvement
activities are actually being used in New Zealand elementary schools. This chapter
reports the findings of two studies of parental involvement in elementary schools in
the Canterbury region of New Zealand. One study focused on urban schools and the
other on rural schools. In order to obtain an international perspective, case studies
of elementary schools in England and Barbados were also carried out and findings
were compared with those from the two New Zealand studies.

The aim of the first study was, therefore, to conduct an exploratory investigation
of school-based parent involvement in rural elementary schools. That is, to find out
which aspects of parental involvement are widely used by schools and to identify
weaknesses or gaps in the provision of parental involvement in these schools, to
highlight implications for practice.

Rural schools, because of their connections with the communities in which they
are based, are considered to have several advantages over urban schools in relation
to school–community partnerships in general and parental involvement in particular (Bauch, 2001; Herzog & Pittman, 1995; Osborne & deOnis, 1997). These
include the social networks created by close school–community bonds, the con-
nectedness and involvement residents feel with their community, increased parent
involvement in all aspects of their children's lives, close ties between church and
school communities, the involvement of community agencies and businesses in
supporting the school, and members of rural communities acting as curricular
resources to schools.

Survey of Parental Involvement in Rural Elementary Schools

Twenty-two elementary schools in rural parts of the Canterbury region, in the south
island of New Zealand, which has a population of approximately 480,000 people,
were surveyed regarding their parental involvement practices (Hornby & Witte,
2010a). Schools were randomly selected by choosing every fifth school on an

alphabetical list of all the 119 elementary schools in the Canterbury region. The 23 schools selected were contacted to arrange interviews with the principals. One principal declined the invitation to be involved, so 22 schools made up the final sample. In 19 of the schools, the principals were interviewed, in one school the deputy principal was interviewed, and in two schools the chairs of the schools' Board of Trustees (BoT) were interviewed. Interviews were conducted at the schools involved and lasted approximately one hour.

Participants

The 22 schools varied in size from 11 to 351 with a mean of 127 children. All schools were coeducational state schools. There were three one-teacher schools (age 5–13 years), eight elementary schools (age 5–11 years), ten full elementary schools (age 5–13 years) and one area school (age 5–18 years). The socioeconomic status (SES) of communities from which schools drew their pupils was estimated using the New Zealand decile system, which involves a ten-point scale on which decile one schools are the 10% of schools that have most pupils from low SES families and decile ten are the 10% of schools that have the most pupils from high SES families. Decile ratings of the 22 schools ranged from two to ten with a mean of 7.86, indicating that the schools were serving communities with a range of SES, but with more schools serving above-average SES communities.

Measures

A structured interview schedule was employed to collect data on participants' views of 11 aspects of parental involvement. It included a list of questions based on the model developed by Hornby (1990) that is elaborated in Chap. 3. The interviews included questions on four aspects of parental involvement concerned with parents' potential contributions to the school, that is, policy formation, acting as a resource, collaboration with teachers, and sharing information on children. It also included questions on four aspects of parental involvement concerned with the needs of parents, that is, the need for channels of communication, liaison with school staff, parent education, and parent support. Additional questions focused on three related aspects of parental involvement, activities for encouraging parents into school, involving diverse parents, and professional development for teachers.

Findings of the Survey

Key findings on each of the 11 aspects of parental involvement are presented below.

Policy Formation

None of the 22 schools had separate written policies on parental involvement. There was a Parent–Teacher Association (PTA) or equivalent at 17 of the schools, but not at the other five schools. Estimates of attendance at PTA meetings ranged from 5 to 50% of parents. Parents were encouraged to become members of the PTA by informal networking at 16 schools, through newsletters at eight schools, through BoT member contacts at seven schools, and through school staff at three schools. Participants reported that parents' views on school policies were sought by means of school newsletters requesting feedback at 17 schools, by informal networking at 12 schools, by questionnaire surveys at nine schools, and via members of the school's BoT at three schools. When asked whether there was a room at the school set aside for parents' use, 11 participants reported that there was not, but nine said parents used the school staff room, and five said they used the school library or hall when they needed a room. Key findings were that none of the schools had written school policies on parental involvement, but the majority did have active PTAs, which, however, typically only involved a minority of parents.

Acting as a Resource

The ways in which parents act as a resource included helping with transport for school or class trips at 15 schools, helping with literacy and numeracy in the classroom at 14 schools, helping with sports activities at 13 schools, helping in other ways in the classroom at eight schools, helping on school camps at five schools, helping with musical, dramatic, or cultural performances at five schools, helping with "pet days" at four schools, preparing teaching materials at two schools, assisting with road crossing patrol before and after school at two schools, helping in the school library at two schools, and helping on school "working Bs" at two schools. Twenty-one participants reported that parents were informed about possible ways of helping at school through school newsletters, 12 through the school prospectus or parent handbook, five through notes sent home with pupils, three through phone calls, two via the PTA, two through the principal, and two via the school Web site. When asked who coordinated voluntary parent help at their schools, 11 schools said that it was left to individual teachers, five said it was done by the principal, and four said it was done by syndicate leaders and five schools indicated that all staff were responsible for this. When asked who was responsible for identifying potential parent volunteers, 14 schools reported that it was up to class teachers, six said it was done by the principal, and five said it was done by BoT members. The wide range of activities in which parents were involved at the schools are an indication that acting as a resource is an important role that parents play in rural schools, as indicated by the literature on parental involvement in rural schools noted earlier (Bauch, 2001; Herzog & Pittman, 1995; Osborne & deOnis, 1997).

Collaborating with Teachers

Results of pupil assessments were communicated to parents through individual parent–teacher meetings at 17 schools, by means of pupil reports in 16 schools, through portfolios of pupils' work in ten schools, by means of parent–teacher–child conferences in seven schools, and at "open-evenings" at two schools. Seven participants reported that input from parents on goals for their children was obtained at parent–teacher meetings, five said this happened at goal-setting conferences, three at IEP meetings, and two at parent–teacher–child conferences. When asked how parents are encouraged to reinforce school programs, 15 schools said that this happened through parents checking homework, six said that newsletters were used for this, and four said that it was done through parents working on literacy or numeracy skills at home. Nine schools reported that teachers exercised flexibility in expectations of parental involvement in homework, whereas 13 said that there was no flexibility. The wide diversity of practice of parental involvement among the schools that emerged from these reports highlighted the fact that important aspects of collaboration were in place in some schools but missing in others. For example, only three schools mentioned involving parents in IEP meetings, whereas all schools would have included children with special educational needs.

Sharing Information on Children

Information on children's special educational needs was obtained from parents during parent–teacher meetings in 16 schools, from previous schools in 13 schools, from standardized enrolment forms in 12 schools, from home visits in three schools, from other professionals (such as itinerant teachers or health nurses visiting the school) in five schools, and from records of the special educational needs coordinator in one school. Dissemination of this information to teachers was achieved at staff meetings in seven schools, through access to student filing/computer systems in six schools, by the principal talking directly with teachers concerned in three schools, via the special needs register in three schools, and through enrolment information being passed directly to teachers in three schools. Clearly, a wide range of mechanisms were used for collecting and disseminating information on pupils. However, it was surprising that, in responding to this section of the interview, none of the 22 participants mentioned sharing information about children's special educational needs through the IEP process.

Channels of Communication

Eighteen schools reported that they communicate with parents through school or class newsletters, 15 schools through the school prospectus, handbook, or enrolment pack, five schools through BoT meetings, four schools via parent–teacher meetings, and three schools via the school Web site. Channels of communication open to parents were reported to be telephone calls (19 schools), notes sent by or to parents (19 schools), meetings by appointment (19 schools), parents dropping in to school (17 schools), e-mail (six schools), text messages (three schools), and informal contacts during pick-up and drop-off of children (three schools). When asked about school policy for contacting teachers if parents have concerns, 14 schools reported that they operated an open-door policy and that parents "dropping in" to school were encouraged. Twelve schools reported that parents were made aware of the school's complaints procedure. Ten schools reported that parents could make appointments to have interviews with teachers. Three schools reported that guidelines for expressing concerns were provided in school newsletters. One school reported that parents could express concerns at IEP meetings. The wide range of ways of communicating with parents used by schools means that parents are able to choose the channels of communication that they prefer, which should lead to optimum overall home–school communication. However, this places high demands on teachers, who must therefore operate a number of different mechanisms for communicating with parents.

Liaison with School Staff

Parent–teacher meetings were held twice a year in 13 schools, whereas three schools reported that this happened four times a year, two schools reported three times a year, and one school reported once a year. Formal reports were sent home twice a year in ten schools, once a year in nine schools, and four times a year in one school. Portfolios of children's work were sent home twice a year in four schools, four times a year in three schools, and three times a year in one school. Home–school diaries were used for pupils with behavior problems in nine schools, for children with special educational needs in four schools, used "as needed" in two schools, and not used at all in six schools. Home visits were reported not to be made to parents at 21 of the schools, whereas one school noted that home visits were made "when needed." The finding that minimal use was made of home visits was surprising since it was expected that, because of the close ties of rural schools to their communities, home visits would be widely used by school staff, particularly for children with special educational needs. Also surprising was the wide range of practice with regard to sending home reports on pupils' progress and portfolios of children's work.

Parent Education

Schools reported that parents were informed about parent education opportunities in the community by means of newsletters at 16 schools, via notice boards at two schools, and through the PTA, BoT, e-mail, and the principal, in one school each. Parent education workshops were not provided in 13 of the schools. Of the other schools, four provided workshops on reading, four on numeracy, and one on education about puberty. Teachers were reported to be available to provide guidance to parents at any time in six schools, during informal discussions with teachers in three schools, after school in three schools, and at parent–teacher interviews in two schools. Ten schools reported that parents were not invited to school to observe teaching, whereas four schools noted that this happened at open days and four reported that the school's open-door policy meant that parents could come to observe teaching at any time. An important finding here was the minimal emphasis evident on parent education, either individually or through parent workshops.

Parent Support

Twelve schools reported that opportunities for parents to obtain support from teachers were provided through informal parent–teacher meetings, 11 schools through formal meetings with teachers, and three schools reported that support was given over telephone calls. Teachers in six schools were reported to have gained knowledge of places to refer parents for support from specialists who visit the school (such as social workers, nurses, and itinerant special education teachers), and from senior staff in eight schools. When asked whether parents were encouraged to join support groups, seven schools reported that this was done through newsletters, and four schools noted that this was done "when needed." Opportunities for parent-to-parent support were not provided in eight schools but were organized in nine schools through informal contacts, and in two schools through parent–teacher meetings. These findings suggest that providing support to parents was not high on the agendas of these rural elementary schools.

Encouraging Parents into School

Schools reported a wide range of activities that were used to encourage parents to establish contact with the school, including performances such as plays or musicals involving many or all of the pupils (21 schools), inviting parents and other family members to view exhibitions of pupils' work (20 schools), inviting parents to attend school or class lunches or barbeques (19 schools), open days or open nights when parents could come and see the school in action (17 schools), talks by invited speakers (14 schools), new parents' evenings (13 schools), and involving parents in sports days (13 schools). In addition, nine schools involved parents in sporting activities, the same number involved parents in "pet days," and nine schools invited parents to attend special assemblies to celebrate pupils' achievements. Eight schools involved parents in school camps, seven in school fairs, and three in class trips. The wide range of activities used by schools to bring about high levels of parental involvement reflect the suggestions found in the now extensive international literature on working with parents (Epstein, 2001; Grant & Ray, 2010; Henderson, Mapp, Johnson, & Davies, 2007). This finding suggests that although most schools are aware of strategies for encouraging parental involvement, the use of these varies from school to school depending on the experiences and views of principals and teachers.

Involving Diverse Parents

Ten schools reported that parents of children with special educational needs were fully involved in the IEP process, ten reported that parents attended IEP meetings, and four said that parents were involved in setting goals for their children. Five schools reported that involvement of parents of gifted children was via extension activities, and two schools said that parents were involved in identifying their children as gifted. Adaptations reported for working with parents from different ethnic groups and/or with English as a second language (ESL) included using interpreters, making home visits, involving them in the PTA, and incorporating different cultures into the curriculum, though these were mentioned by only one school each. It is clear that having a range of strategies for involving parents from ethnically diverse backgrounds was not evident in the schools.

Professional Development for Teachers

It was reported that there had been no training for teachers on working with parents at 14 of the schools, but four said there had been some in-service training on parental involvement, with two of these saying that this had focused on interpersonal skills and conflict resolution. Two schools reported that mentoring of teachers on parental involvement was provided by senior staff, and a further two said that internet resources on parental involvement were utilized. When asked whether parents were involved in professional development sessions for teachers, 17 schools reported that this had not occurred, but four said that it had been done when children had diabetes, autism, Asperger's syndrome, or dyslexia. So, it is clear that professional development on parental involvement for teachers in these 22 schools was extremely limited.

Discussion of Findings

It appears that all of the 22 rural elementary schools used a range of activities in which they involved parents. There was, however, a wide diversity of practice of parental involvement in these schools. There were very few parental involvement activities that all schools used and few types of parental involvement specified in the survey questionnaire that no schools were involved in. There were many examples of parental involvement practice in individual schools that are recommended in the literature, but these were not consistent across all schools and the overall picture was patchy. The most notable weaknesses in parental involvement provision in the schools were, a lack of written school policies, minimal use of home visits, limited ideas to involve diverse parents, minimal parent education organized by schools, minimal focus on parent support, the ad hoc nature of the organization of parental involvement, minimal focus on involving parents of children with special educational needs, and limited training for teachers on working with parents. These weaknesses are discussed below.

A key weakness was that none of the schools had written school policies on parental involvement, whereas it is suggested in the literature on parental involvement that all schools should develop written policies which set out the ways in which parents can be involved in their children's education, as well as the procedures through which schools and teachers can help parents to accomplish this (Epstein, 2001; Henderson et al., 2007). It is also recommended that policies for parental involvement should be developed in collaboration with parents, such as members of the PTA, to ensure that the activities included will meet the needs of the different communities in which schools are based.

The finding that there was minimal use of home visits by school staff indicates underuse of one aspect of parental involvement that many parents appreciate, particularly those with children who have special educational needs. Home visits can be very helpful for teachers in building rapport with parents and gaining understanding of children's home circumstances (Grant & Ray, 2010). It is, therefore, important for schools to attempt to overcome difficulties related to home visits, such as time constraints, issues of personal safety, and some teachers' diffidence in relating to parents, to make use of this aspect of involving parents when it is appropriate.

Another important finding was the lack of specific ideas to involve parents from ethnically diverse backgrounds. Schools in New Zealand, as in many other countries around the world, are becoming more ethnically diverse. Many parents have English as a second language and come from countries with traditional schooling systems in which parental involvement is not emphasized and, therefore, expect to have little involvement with their children's schools. It is essential for schools to reach out to such parents so that they appreciate the importance of their involvement in their children's education. Therefore, schools need to work hard to develop innovative ways to involve these parents (Grant & Ray, 2010; Henderson et al., 2007).

It is clear that parent education organized by schools was not seen as a priority, and referral of parents to parent education sessions available in the community was patchy. Without appropriate parent education, family members may not fully appreciate the importance of getting involved with their children's schools and also fail to provide the kind of support at home that will optimize children's academic achievements (Epstein, 2001).

The finding of a minimal focus on parent support was another weakness identified. It is considered that teachers should be able to provide support to parents in terms of basic counseling and guidance regarding their children's learning and behavior as well as being able to refer parents who need more intensive help to appropriate sources of support that are available in their communities (Grant & Ray, 2010). It is, therefore, important that teachers learn basic counseling and guidance skills as part of their initial training or through ongoing professional development courses (Turnbull, Turnbull, Erwin, Soodak, & Shogren, 2011).

The overall organization of parental involvement in the schools appeared ad hoc and very much dependent on the views and experience of principals and other senior staff. As Epstein and Salinas (2004) suggest, what is needed in schools is a comprehensive system of parental involvement that includes all key aspects. In order to achieve this, it is suggested that elementary schools need to have a parental involvement coordinator who is an experienced teacher or member of the school's senior management team. The first job of the parental involvement coordinator should be to conduct an audit of parental involvement at the school and prepare a report for the school's principal and governing body to facilitate the development of a comprehensive system for parental involvement at the school.

Findings also highlight the lack of a specific focus on involving parents of children with special educational needs in these rural elementary schools. Similar to children with special educational needs, such parents have many needs in common with their peers, but there are some areas where their needs, and what they can contribute, do differ from those of other parents. For example, they need to be fully involved in their children's IEPs so that they can contribute their in-depth knowledge of their children's difficulties and strengths, as well as discuss goals and priorities for the future (Seligman & Darling, 2007). Parents of children with special educational needs also require frequent and effective communication to be in place between school and home, such as through the use of home–school diaries so that any issues or concerns that occur, either at school or at home, can be quickly addressed.

The finding that there was such limited training for teachers on working with parents is alarming and suggests that the success of government initiatives on improving parental involvement (e.g., MoE, 2005) may be limited until this situation changes. Teacher education programs need to include rigorous courses on working with parents for preservice teachers, and ongoing professional development should be provided for practicing teachers. Training should be focused on enabling teachers to be confident implementing the wide range of aspects of parental involvement that is found to be useful by schools and parents. Despite the content of teacher education programs in New Zealand (as in other countries) being specified by government education policies (which include those promoting parental involvement) as noted above (MoE), there is still no requirement to include comprehensive courses on working with parents in teacher education programs. The importance of such courses for providing teachers with the skills to work effectively with parents has been acknowledged internationally (Epstein, 2001; Greenwood & Hickman, 1991). As government policies do not require these courses, they are typically not included or, as in the USA where accreditation standards do require them, are not considered rigorous enough to ensure that teachers are adequately prepared to work effectively with parents (Flanigan, 2007). It is therefore important that teacher education courses prepare teachers to involve parents in a wide range of parental involvement activities, including introducing teachers to a range of strategies for involving parents from diverse backgrounds, preparing teachers for their role in educating parents about optimizing their children's development, as well as training teachers to address the specific needs of parents and families of children with special educational needs.

This survey has highlighted many areas of parental involvement practice in this sample of rural elementary schools in New Zealand that are in line with those suggested in the international literature. In order to find out whether these findings were also the case for urban schools in New Zealand, a further survey was conducted.

Survey of Parental Involvement in Urban Elementary Schools

A survey was also conducted of the practice of parental involvement in 21 elementary schools in Christchurch, a city of around 400,000 people in the south island of New Zealand (Hornby & Witte, 2010b). The schools were randomly selected by choosing every fifth school on an alphabetical list of the 116 primary schools. The 22 schools selected were contacted to arrange interviews with the principals. One principal declined the invitation to be involved, so 21 schools made up the final sample. The 21 schools varied in size from 53 to 551 with a mean of 273 children. All schools were coeducational public (not private) schools. Decile ratings of the 21 schools ranged from one to ten with a mean of 5.38, indicating that the schools were serving communities with a broad range of SES. Principals were interviewed at their schools with interviews lasting approximately one hour.

Findings were very similar to those from rural elementary schools in that a wide diversity of practice of parental involvement was also found in these urban schools. Once again, many examples of parental involvement practices were found in individual schools that are recommended in the literature, but these were not consistent across all schools and the overall picture was patchy. The most notable weaknesses in parental involvement provision in the schools were, once again, a lack of written school policies, minimal use of home visits, limited ideas to involve diverse parents, minimal focus on parent education and parent support, the ad hoc nature of the organization of parental involvement, minimal focus on involving parents of children with special needs, and limited training for teachers on working with parents (see Hornby & Witte, 2010b).

Case Studies of English and Barbadian Schools

In order to gain some degree of international comparison, principals at two elementary schools, one in England and one in Barbados, were interviewed using the same interview schedule used in the two New Zealand studies. The English school had a roll of 215 students, and the Barbadian school had a roll of 146 students. Both schools were located in urban areas in communities of predominantly lower SES levels. Both principals were highly experienced educators, known personally to the author. However, whereas the English school operated in an education system that strongly encourages and expects high levels of parent involvement, the Barbadian education system is a much more traditional one, in which home–school collaboration is not expected by either parents or teachers. Findings from the interviews are summarized below.

English Elementary School

Policy Formation

The school does not have a written policy for parental involvement. It does have an active PTA, but only a handful of parents attend PTA meetings, which tend to be social in nature and focused on fund-raising, although events organized by the PTA are well attended. There is no room set aside for parents use, but parent volunteers use the library and parents use the staff room at break time. Parents' views about school policies and procedures are sought by means of questionnaires and consultation at parent–teacher evenings. Parents are encouraged to join the PTA and Board of Governors by current members and by promotion of this at open days and other school events.

Acting as a Resource

Parents are informed about ways they can help at school through newsletters and a leaflet on parent help displayed in the school foyer. Parents help by listening to children read, working in the school library, and providing help in teaching sewing and cooking. The principal and inclusion teacher/manager coordinate parent helpers, but class teachers provide day-to-day supervision.

Collaborating with Teachers

Assessments of children's academic progress are communicated to parents through assessment sheets with grades for English, math, behavior, attendance, and extra-curricular activities, sent home every term, as well as formal reports sent out at the end of the year. Parent–teacher meetings are held twice a year. Parents are encouraged to support school programs through home–school agreements, home–school diaries, and reading logs.

Sharing Information on Children

Information on children's special educational needs is obtained from contacts with previous schools and parent–teacher meetings. This information is shared with teachers at planning meetings. Parents' insights on their children are reported to be used as much as possible, particularly in the early years.

Channels of Communication

A parent handbook is used to inform parents of their rights and responsibilities. Use is also made of the school notice board, Web site, e-mails, and leaflets written especially for parents. Families are not visited before children start school. The school operates an "open-door" policy so that parents with concerns can either mention this when they pick up children or phone or e-mail teachers. Another channel of communication is notes in home–school diaries.

Liaison with School Staff

Parent–teacher meetings are held mid year and toward the end of the year. Home visits are rare and, if necessary, are made by health visitors (nurses who visit schools). Home–school diaries are used with all children and focus on reading, spelling, and, for children with behavior problems, a daily behavior report to be signed by parents.

Parent Education

Teachers are available to provide guidance to parents at parent–teacher meetings. Ideas for parent education courses and workshops are displayed on the school notice board. Workshops are organized for parents of children in the early years and those about to transition to high school.

Parent Support

Parents can discuss their concerns with teachers at specially scheduled parent–teacher meetings and with the principal over telephone. The inclusion teacher/manager refers parents to community agencies for guidance and counseling when necessary.

Encouraging Parents into School

The school uses open days, new parents evenings, school performances, and school barbeques to encourage parents to come into the school. The school's "open-door" policy is explained at the new parents evening. Teachers are available before and after school to talk with parents.

Involving Diverse Parents

The principal and inclusion teacher/manager put a lot of effort into building rela-tionships with ethnic minority parents. Parents are fully involved in IEPs for children with special educational needs. Parents of gifted children are informed that their children have been selected for involvement in extension programs.

Professional Development for Teachers

Teachers at the school have had only informal in-service training on working with parents. Parents of children with cochlea implants and feeding problems have provided some input into this training.

Barbadian Elementary School

Policy Formation

The school does not have a written policy for parental involvement but does have an active PTA with up to 25 parents involved in monthly meetings. There is no room set aside for parents use. Parents' views are not sought about school policies or procedures because this is "not regarded as the parents' role."

Acting as a Resource

Parents are informed about ways they can help at the school through PTA meetings, but parent volunteering is not a part of the culture of the school, so it is minimal. The school does not send out newsletters to parents.

Collaborating with Teachers

Assessments of children's academic progress are communicated to parents through end-of-term reports and at parent–teacher meetings held once a year. Parent support of school programs is through an expectation that parents encourage their children to do the homework that is set.

Sharing Information on Children

Information on children's special educational needs is obtained from enrolment forms and yearly parent–teacher meetings and is stored on record cards in the school office, where this can be accessed by teachers. It is noted that although the principal encourages teachers to ask parents for any insights on their children, parents do not share much of this with teachers.

Channels of Communication

A parent handbook is used to inform parents of their rights and responsibilities. Families are not visited before children start school. The school operates an "open-door" policy so that parents with concerns can either drop in or phone or write notes. They are expected to talk with the principal first, then class teachers. The principal encourages teachers to phone parents to provide positive feedback on children's achievements or behavior.

Liaison with School Staff

Reports are sent home three times a year and parent–teacher meetings are held yearly. The principal makes home visits if parents cannot be contacted about children's progress. Home–school diaries are not used.

Parent Education

Teachers are available to provide guidance to parents at parent–teacher meetings. Ideas for parent education courses and workshops are shared at PTA meetings. The principal was currently planning a full day workshop for parents, with various speakers, to be held on a Saturday.

Parent Support

Parents can discuss their concerns with teachers at parent–teacher meetings and with other parents at PTA meetings. The principal refers parents to community agencies for guidance and counseling, when necessary.

Encouraging Parents into School

The PTA organizes a "meet and greet" session once a year so that parents can meet other parents, and at the time of the interview, the PTA was planning a "fish-fry" to encourage parents to come in to the school. The school does not use open days, new parents evenings, school performances, exhibitions of children's work, talks by invited speakers or school fairs to encourage parents to come in to the school.

Involving Diverse Parents

The school has families who have come from different islands in the Caribbean but does not do anything special to involve parents from diverse backgrounds, as it is considered that they all speak English. Parents are not involved in IEPs for children with special educational needs, or in extension programs for gifted children, or in reviews of their children's progress.

Professional Development for Teachers

Teachers at the school have had no training, either preservice or in-service, on working with parents.

Comparison of Parental Involvement in English and Barbadian Schools

Stark differences are evident between the range and amount of parental involvement in the two schools. For example, the English school uses a wide range of activities to encourage parental involvement, such as open days, new parents evenings, and school performances, whereas the Barbadian school uses none of these. In addition, home–school diaries are used with all children in the English school but not at all in the Barbadian school. Also, newsletters to parents are not used in the Barbadian school, but are seen as a key means for home–school communication in the English school. Further, voluntary help from parents in a wide range of activities is evident in the English school but almost completely lacking in the Barbadian one. In contrast, whereas home visits are not seen as the responsibility of staff in the English school, they are regarded as within role of the principal at the Barbadian school.

When visiting the two schools to conduct the interviews, it was clear that the foyer of the English school was very welcoming to parents, with chairs for them to sit on while they were waiting to talk to staff and leaflets available on issues of interest to parents for them to read or take away with them. The Barbadian school, although recently built, had no obvious reception area for parents.

The low level of parental involvement at the Barbadian school is not considered to be due to a lack of interest or motivation on the part of the principal, since she had undergone training on working with parents as part of her Masters degree and is enthusiastic about involving parents, as is illustrated by the Saturday workshop and "fish-fry" she was planning at the time of the interview. Alternatively, it seems that a broad range of the barriers discussed in Chap. 2 were influencing the quality and quantity of parental involvement at the school at that time. Such factors as negative societal attitudes to parental involvement and minimal parental expectations of involvement, typical in Barbadian culture, are influential and will take considerable work and time to overcome.

Summary and Conclusion

Elementary schools in New Zealand, England, and Barbados were surveyed regarding their practice of parental involvement. A wide range of activities were found to be used by schools to involve parents. There was, however, a wide diversity of practice of parental involvement in the schools with few activities that all schools used and few types of involvement identified that no schools were involved in. Several common weaknesses in parental involvement practices were identified: a lack of written school policies on parental involvement, the ad hoc nature of the organization of parental involvement, limited parent education and parent support activities, minimal use of home visits, limited ideas to involve diverse parents, a minimal focus on involving parents of children with special educational needs, and limited professional development for teachers on working with parents. Guidelines for implementing the major parental involvement practices that have been identified in this chapter as needing more consistent implementation across schools are discussed in Chap. 6.

Chapter 5
Parental Involvement in Middle and Secondary Schools

Introduction

A key finding from the literature on parental involvement is that its effectiveness in bringing about improvements in children's social and academic achievements holds across ethnicity, gender, and age of the children involved (Eccles & Harold, 1993; Jeynes, 2007). Most of the literature on parental involvement focuses on elementary schools, but the involvement of parents is still regarded as important at secondary school (Wheeler, 1992), and it is widely acknowledged that "Parental involvement has a significant effect on pupil achievement throughout the years of schooling" (DCFS, 2007, p. 5). However, evidence suggests that parental involvement tends to decline throughout the middle school and secondary school years (Hill et al., 2004; Hoover-Dempsey et al., 2005; Spera, 2005). There are at least three possible reasons for this (Chen, 2008; Christenson, 2004). First, middle and secondary schools may not be as welcoming to parents as elementary schools are. Second, parents may be less confident being involved in their children's education since subject material becomes more challenging as their children progress through middle and secondary schools. Third, as children negotiate adolescence and attempt to become more autonomous, they may be less open to having parents involved with their schools.

Nevertheless, parental involvement at secondary school level has been found to be an important predictor of school outcomes throughout adolescence (Hill & Taylor, 2004; Hoover-Dempsey et al., 2005). For example, Deslandes and Cloutier (2002) found that when parents are involved in their children's education, secondary students achieve better academically, develop higher aspirations, and exhibit fewer discipline problems. In their study of 872 fourteen-year-olds in the USA, they found that over three quarters of the adolescents were willing to show their parents what they learned or did well on at school. They were also willing to ask parents for ideas for projects, listen to parents tell them about when they were teenagers, and take home notes, notices, and newsletters, whereas, two thirds of teenagers did not want their parents to visit their classes or go on school trips. Thus, it seems that as children grow older, the type of parental involvement changes and parents become

G. Hornby, *Parental Involvement in Childhood Education: Building Effective School-Family Partnerships*, DOI 10.1007/978-1-4419-8379-4_5,
© Springer Science+Business Media, LLC 2011

less directly involved with schools, but are potentially able to become more involved in supportive roles at home, for example, helping with homework, subject choices, and career options (Hill & Taylor). This may explain the finding that parental involvement at middle and secondary schools is associated with increased time students spend on homework (Hill & Taylor).

A recent study of parental involvement conducted in 20 secondary schools in England (Harris & Goodall, 2008) found that parents, teachers, and pupils agree that parental involvement is important but differ in their views about its purpose. It was also found that powerful social and economic forces were acting as barriers to parental involvement. Harris and Goodall report that secondary schools tended to focus on school-based parental involvement and paid insufficient attention to encouraging home-based parental involvement, which is at least as important for secondary school students. They conclude: "It is what parents do to support learning in the school and in the home that makes the difference to achievement" (p. 278). A good example of this is provided by Clark's (1983) study of high-achieving secondary school students from poor Afro-American families. This identified key parenting practices that distinguished parents of high-achieving students from parents of low-achieving students. Parents of highly achieving students reported valuing education, visiting schools and advocating for their children, developing pride and self-reliance in their children, establishing routines for homework and bedtime, supervising children's TV viewing, encouraging reading, talking with their children, playing games with children, taking children on visits and outings, and fostering hobbies, as well as sporting and other activities. So, the parents of successful students in this study were involved in their children's education both at school and home.

Since research suggests that more effective parental involvement, and therefore bigger effect sizes for its impact on student achievement, are obtained for the involvement that schools have organized themselves, rather than externally imposed home–school programs (Pomerantz, Moorman, & Litwack, 2007), it is important to investigate the specific ways in which schools encourage parental involvement, both at school and home. Guidance on provision for parental involvement that is found useful can then be based on evidence from actual practice in schools.

Given the findings of the international literature, it was considered timely to investigate what parental involvement activities are actually found in New Zealand middle and secondary schools. This chapter reports the findings of studies of parental involvement in middle schools and secondary schools in the Canterbury region of New Zealand. In addition, to obtain an international perspective, case studies of secondary schools in England and Barbados were also carried out and findings compared with those from the two New Zealand studies.

Survey of Parental Involvement in Secondary Schools

The aim of the first study was, therefore, to conduct an investigation of parent involvement in secondary schools, that is, to find out which aspects of parental involvement are widely used by schools and to identify weaknesses or gaps in the provision of parental involvement in these schools, in order to highlight implications for practice. A survey of parental involvement in secondary schools was conducted in the Canterbury region of New Zealand, which has a population of approximately 480,000 people (Hornby & Witte, 2010c).

Participants

Twenty-six schools were randomly selected from the 47 secondary schools in the Canterbury region and contacted in order to arrange interviews with principals. Five principals declined the invitation to be involved, so 21 schools made up the final sample. These included a range of types of schools serving rural, urban, and suburban areas. Schools ranged in size from approximately 400 to 1,600 students. The sample included single-sex and coeducational schools, religious schools that were integrated into the state system, and schools that offered an alternative or progressive secondary education. Principals were interviewed at their schools, with interviews lasting from approximately 30 to 60 minutes.

Measures

A structured interview schedule was used to conduct the interviews. The schedule focused on 11 aspects of parental involvement. It included a list of questions adapted from a model developed by Hornby (1990). The interview included questions on four aspects of parental involvement concerned with parents' potential contributions to the school, that is, policy formation, acting as a resource, collaboration with teachers, and sharing information on children. It also included questions on four aspects of parental involvement concerned with the needs of parents, that is, the need for channels of communication, liaison with school staff, parent education, and parent support. Additional questions focused on three related aspects of parental involvement, activities for encouraging parents into school, involving diverse parents, and teacher professional development.

Findings of the Survey

Key findings on each of the 11 aspects of parental involvement surveyed are presented below.

Policy Formation

Only one out of the 21 schools had a separate written policy on parental involvement. Fifteen of the schools had a Parent–Teacher Association (PTA). Estimates from principals about the proportion of parents involved in PTAs varied from 40% to less than 1% of the parent population, and numbers attending PTA meetings varied from 10 to 100 parents. Parents were encouraged to become members of the PTA through contact with existing members of the PTA or Board of Trustees (BoT) (12 schools), suggestions from staff (10 schools), new pupil evenings (eight schools), newsletters (five schools), and open nights (two schools). Principals reported that parents' views on school policies were sought by school newsletters (14 schools), through questionnaire surveys (six schools), via PTA or BoT members (four schools), by focus groups (two schools), and by open nights (two schools). One principal reported that the school had a room for the use of Pacifica parents, another said that a parents' room was being set up, and 19 said that there was no room assigned for the use of parents.

Acting as a Resource

Ways in which parents act as a resource included helping with sports coaching or sports events held at school (15 schools), involvement in cultural/musical or drama events (nine schools), fund-raising (six schools), helping in the school library (four schools), supporting learning (four schools), taking part in working B's (three schools), mentoring pupils (two schools), helping on school camps (two schools), helping on class trips (two schools), working in the school canteen (two schools), and making tea at school functions (two schools). Responsibility for encouraging parents to get involved was reported to be the BoT (six schools), the PTA (five schools), teachers (five schools), a senior management team (four schools), community links (three schools), the principal (two schools), and a database of parent strengths (two schools). All 21 principals reported that parents were informed about possible ways of volunteering at school through school newsletters, five principals said that it was done during the enrolment interview, four said that it was via the school Web site, three through parent handbooks, three via letters sent home, one via e-mails, and one through PTA contacts. When asked who coordinated parent help at their schools, seven principals said that it was done by individual teachers, four said that it was done by the sports coordinator, three principals said that it was done by the PTA, and two principals said that they did it themselves.

Collaborating with Teachers

The results of pupil assessments were communicated to parents through individual parent–teacher meetings at all 22 schools. Nine schools had one meeting a year, six had two, two schools had two or three meetings, another had four meetings, and three schools did not specify the number of meetings. The results of pupil assessments were also communicated to parents through pupil reports at 18 of the schools. Twelve schools had three reports a year, four schools had two reports, one had two or three reports, and another had four reports a year. In four schools, the results of pupil assessments were communicated to parents by means of individual letters or booklets sent home. Four principals reported that parents were involved in assessments and reviews of their children's special educational needs (SEN) through individualized education plans (IEPs). Supervision of children's homework was reported to be the way that parents reinforced school programs at nine schools. Seven principals said that there was flexibility in the school's expectations of parental involvement in homework, while 11 principals said that there was no flexibility.

Sharing Information on Children

Principals reported that information on children's SEN was obtained from parents through parent–teacher meetings (16 schools), enrolment questionnaires (9 schools), enrolment interviews (7 schools), and from home visits by deans or counselors (8 schools). Seventeen principals noted that such information was also obtained from feeder schools. Dissemination of this information to teachers was achieved via the school's pastoral care (PC) system (nine schools), via computerized PC databases (nine schools), through school records (five schools), via talking with deans or senior staff (four schools), at staff meetings (four schools), at PC meetings (two schools), via a health or SEN register (three schools), through e-mails to teachers (three schools), and via the school nurse (two schools). Comments by principals about the use made of parents' information on their children included those that parents' views were listened to (five schools), that this was up to deans (three schools), and that this information was only used when problems arise (two schools).

Channels of Communication

Fifteen schools were reported to use newsletters to communicate with parents. For three schools, communication mainly occurred during enrolment, for another three it was via information provided by the BoT, and for a further three via the school's website. Two schools had used parent handbooks for this, two sent letters home, and two had parent forums. Channels of communication open to parents were letters or notes sent to and from school (20 schools), telephone calls (19 schools), meetings at school by appointment (16 schools), parents dropping in to school (11 schools), e-mail (12 schools), text messages (five schools), homework diaries (three schools), and the school website (two schools). When asked about school policy for contacting teachers if parents had concerns, seven principals reported that parents could contact teachers directly for appointments, and four said that the open-door policy meant that parents were encouraged to drop in to the school at any time. Six principals noted that parents were made aware of the complaints procedure. Five said that the school newsletter and one noted that the school handbook made it clear to parents who to contact if they had a concern. With regard to having balanced procedures for contacting parents, eight principals noted that their schools had student award schemes, two had special assemblies to which parents were invited, and in one school the BoT sent out letters acknowledging students' achievements.

Liaison with School Staff

Principals at 19 schools reported that home visits were not made by teachers, whereas two principals noted that teachers made home visits to parents of students with SEN. Principals at five schools reported that home visits were only made in exceptional circumstances and were carried out by deans or guidance counselors. Homework diaries were used for all students in 12 schools, and home–school diaries were used for some SEN children in nine schools. Other means of reporting to parents used were report cards on attitudes and behavior (three schools), and SEN notebooks (three schools).

Parent Education

Principals reported that parents were informed about parent education opportunities available in the community by means of school newsletters at 11 schools, through associated community education centers at nine schools, and through local newspapers at two schools. Occasional parent education workshops were held at 16 of the schools. Topics included health, sexuality, drug abuse, children with SEN, values, relationships, anxiety, parenting teenagers, curricula, literacy, and study skills. Teachers were reported to be available to provide guidance to parents by appointment at 12 schools and anytime at three schools. Seven principals noted that deans and guidance counselors were also available to provide guidance to parents. Five principals reported that parents were invited to school to observe teaching, 13 principals said they were not and 2 principals said that this occurred on specific occasions, such as open days.

Parent Support

Nine principals reported that opportunities for parents to obtain support from teachers was provided through parent–teacher meetings and eight said that it was done by telephone. Four principals reported that support was available though meetings with deans, another four through meetings with guidance counselors, two through parent workshops, and two through home visits. Teachers were reported to have gained knowledge of places to refer parents for support from guidance counselors (eight schools), from other members of pastoral care teams, such as deans (seven schools), via community groups (four schools), and through church groups (two schools). When asked whether parents were encouraged to join support groups, eight principals said that it was done, and the mechanisms were school newsletters (two schools), church groups (two schools), and guidance counselors (one school). Opportunities for parent-to-parent support were suggested by guidance counselors at three schools, by the PTA at two schools, and "huis" (Maori meetings) at two schools.

Encouraging Parents into School

Schools reported using a range of activities to encourage parents to establish contact with the school. All 21 schools used "open days" when parents could visit the school to see classes in action, "school performances" such as plays that involved many of the pupils and "new parents' evenings" when parents of newly enrolled pupils could look around the school and find out more about how the school functioned. Nineteen of the schools invited parents to see exhibitions of work done by pupils. Seventeen schools had occasional talks for parents by invited speakers. Fifteen schools had school or class lunches or barbeques that parents were invited to attend. Cultural or musical events were used by 11 schools and sporting events by 10 schools to involve parents. Newsletters were used by ten schools to encourage parental involvement, whereas six schools used their websites and email, and four schools used "information evenings" for this purpose. Four schools had annual school fairs that many parents participated in. Three principals reported that they found "report evenings," another three "personalized invitations," and a further three "phoning home" useful for getting parents involved.

Involving Diverse Parents

Nine principals reported involving their local ethnic communities by means of parent groups for Maori, Pacifica, Indian, and refugee parents. Five principals reported that their schools had appointed directors of international education. Twelve principals reported that parents of children with SEN were involved in the IEP process, seven said that learning support coordinators helped to involve parents, and five said that links with agencies for SEN children were used to facilitate the involvement of parents. Adaptations reported for working with parents with English as a second language (ESL) were: the ESL teacher working with children and parents (seven schools), using interpreters (nine schools), translating newsletters into different languages (six schools), help from Samoan speakers (three schools), and teacher aides (three schools). Adaptations for involving parents of gifted children included having a gifted student coordinator (eight schools), involving parents in extension activities (four schools) and individual parent–teacher interviews (two schools).

Teacher Professional Development

Eight principals reported that there had been minimal preservice training for teachers on parental involvement, and five said that none had occurred in-service. Three principals said that some training was done as part of the induction of new teachers, another three said that some training in working with parents was done before parent–teacher interviews, and two said that role modeling was provided by senior staff. One principal reported that professional development on working with parents was provided at the school and this involved role plays of face-to-face and phone contacts with parents. When asked whether parents were involved in professional development sessions for teachers, 15 principals said that this did not happen, three said that it did, and two said that it was done with parents of special needs or gifted students.

Discussion of Findings

A wide diversity in the practice of parental involvement was found in the 21 secondary schools. There were some aspects of parental involvement that all schools used, and many examples of effective parental involvement practices, but these were not consistent across all schools. Some innovative practices were found, for example, student award schemes used to provide positive feedback to parents on students' achievements, and schools using new technology such as school websites and e-mails to communicate with parents. The most notable gaps were the absence of written school policies on parental involvement, the ad hoc nature of the organization of parental involvement by schools, the lack of specific ideas to involve parents from diverse backgrounds, the limited focus on parent education, and the minimal training for teachers on working with parents at both preservice and in-service levels.

The finding that only one of the 21 secondary schools had a written policy on parental involvement suggests that policy for parental involvement is paid insufficient attention in these schools and therefore that there may be a lack of clarity about parental involvement policy and practice in the schools. It is considered that all schools should develop written policies on parental involvement and that this should be done in collaboration with parents, such as members of the PTA. Policies should set out all the different ways in which parents can be involved in their children's education, both at school and home, as well as the procedures through which schools can help parents to accomplish this.

As with the elementary schools surveyed, the diversity of practice among these secondary schools highlighted important aspects of parental involvement that were in place at some schools but missing at others. Overall organization of parental involvement in the schools appeared ad hoc and very much related to the views and experience of principals. As Epstein and Salinas (2004) suggest, what is needed in schools is a comprehensive system of parental involvement, which includes key aspects of parental involvement such as those highlighted in this chapter. In order to achieve this, it is suggested that secondary schools need to have a parental involvement coordinator who is an experienced teacher or a member of the school's senior management team. The first task of the parental involvement coordinator should be to conduct an audit of parental involvement at the school and prepare a report for the school's principal and governors in order to facilitate the development of a comprehensive system for parental involvement at the school. Schools should regularly review the state of parental involvement in their schools to facilitate its ongoing implementation and development.

An important finding was that some parent education workshops and lectures were organized by schools but the topics addressed were limited and referral of parents to parent education sessions available in the community was patchy. As stated earlier, when children move from primary to secondary schools, the way in which parents are involved in their education changes (Chen, 2008; Hill & Taylor, 2004). Involvement of parents at school becomes less important, while involvement at home, such as in supervising homework and advising on subject option choices, becomes more important. Without appropriate parent education parents may not realize this and fail to provide the kind of support at home that will optimize their children's academic achievements (Hoover-Dempsey et al., 2005).

Another finding similar to that from the survey of elementary schools reported in the previous chapter was the lack of specific strategies for involving parents from ethnically diverse backgrounds. Secondary schools in New Zealand, as in many other countries around the world, are becoming more ethnically diverse. Many parents have English as a second language or come from countries with traditional schooling systems in which parental involvement is not emphasized and therefore find it difficult to get involved with their children's schools. It is essential for schools to reach out to such parents so that they can appreciate the importance of their involvement to their children's education (ERO, 2008). Therefore, schools need to work hard to develop innovative ways to involve these parents.

The finding that there was limited training of teachers on working with parents, both preservice and in-service, suggests that the success of government initiatives focusing on improving parental involvement in children's education may be limited until this situation changes. Governments need to ensure that training on parental involvement is a mandatory part of teacher education both preservice and in-service. Teacher education programs need to include rigorous courses on working with parents and ongoing professional development on parental involvement must be provided for practicing teachers (Koutrouba, Antonopoulou, Tsitsas, & Zenakou, 2009). Training needs to be focused on enabling teachers to be confident using the wide range of aspects of parental involvement that have been found, in this survey, to be used in schools.

As suggested in Chap. 1, Pelco et al (2000) have suggested that psychologists have a key role to play in the in-service training of teachers for parental involvement. For example, psychologists can help teachers develop effective communication skills for use with parents, as well as techniques for organizing effective parent–teacher conferences. Psychologists can also encourage teachers to make home visits to families who would appreciate this. In addition to their training and guidance of teachers, psychologists can work with parents of children at all ages to ensure that they have the information they need to use effective home-based parental involvement and for collaborating effectively with schools. For example, psychologists can help parents develop strategies for conveying higher educational aspirations to their children. Psychologists can also encourage the involvement of extended family members in home-based and school-based parental involvement. Pelco et al. make the point that psychologists must advocate for parental involvement programs that are integral to the school's educational mission rather than short-term, add-on programs that are likely to be less effective. In these ways, psychologists have a key role to play in promoting and facilitating family-school partnerships.

The study reported above has highlighted some areas of good practice as well as some important gaps regarding parental involvement in the 21 secondary schools. However, in the final analysis, the key to effective parental involvement is probably the willingness of school principals and teachers to do everything they can to actively engage the parents of all students in their children's education. Many school psychologists, counselors, social workers, and other professionals who work with schools have the specialist knowledge and skills to help school principals and teachers to develop an ethos in which this becomes a reality. It is essential that these professionals recognize this and are prepared to fulfill the important role of providing leadership and support to schools to bring about effective parental involvement.

Parental Involvement in Middle Schools

The literature suggests that as children make the transition from elementary to secondary schools, the type of parental involvement changes, as noted earlier. Parents become less directly involved with schools but more involved in supportive roles at home, for example, helping children with homework and advising on subject option choices (Hill & Taylor, 2004). However, the literature also indicates that developmentally appropriate parental involvement remains associated with positive student outcomes throughout the middle and secondary school years (Hoover-Dempsey et al., 2005).

In their study of three middle schools and five primary schools in the USA, Epstein and Dauber (1991) found that programs of parental involvement were weaker and less comprehensive at middle schools than at primary schools. So parents were receiving less information and guidance on how to be involved with their children's education at the very time that they were trying to cope with the changing type and complexity of parental involvement with their middle-school age children.

In fact, Elias, Patrikakou, and Weissberg (2007) have suggested that parental involvement is particularly important at middle school because this is the time when children are making the transition to adolescence as well as the transition from elementary school to secondary education. They argue that evidence for many children finding these transitions difficult is provided by the fact that middle school is the time of peak referral for mental health problems. They emphasize the importance of effective parental involvement at this time when they state, "...middle school transition and establishing a positive trajectory into the teen years require a parent–school–community partnership..." (p. 542).

Hayes and Chodkiewicz (2006) also consider school–community links to be particularly important for children in the middle years of schooling because of the increased incidence of pupil disengagement from school in these years.

They studied school–community relationships at four Australian schools in order to identify links in place to support the engagement of pupils in the middle years. They found that the schools viewed school–community links as important and were all involved in attempting to improve the involvement of parents.

Prompted by the above, a survey of parental involvement in middle schools was conducted in Christchurch, which is a city of around 400,000 people, in the South Island of New Zealand (Hornby & Witte, 2010d). In New Zealand, around 50% of children spend 2 years at middle schools, which are typically called intermediate schools, between attending elementary and secondary school. These children start school at the age of 5 years and spend years 1–6 in primary schools, years 7 and 8 in middle schools (at ages 11–13 years), and years 9–13 in secondary schools. The other 50% of children either stay in primary schools for years 7 and 8 or start secondary school in year 7, depending on the schools available in their area in which they live and parents' choice of school.

Survey

Principals at each of the 11 intermediate (middle) schools in Christchurch were contacted, and all agreed to be interviewed. Ten principals were interviewed by a research associate, at their schools, during the final few weeks of the school year and the 11th at his home during the school holidays. Interviews lasted between 30 and 90 min. The study sample, therefore, comprised all 11 middle schools in the city. All schools were coeducational and ranged in size from 188 to 820 pupils with a mean of 416.

Findings were similar to those from secondary schools regarding the various forms of parental involvement that schools were involved in and typical gaps in parental involvement policy and practices. Similar to secondary schools, the most important gaps were considered to be the absence of written school policies on parental involvement, the ad hoc nature of the organization of parental involvement by schools, the lack of specific ideas to involve parents from diverse backgrounds, the limited focus on parent education, and the minimal training for teachers on working with parents at both preservice and in-service levels.

The major difference identified was the finding that there was less use of home visits by school staff at middle schools than at the secondary schools. Whereas 8 out of the 21 secondary schools reported using home visits, only 2 out of the 11 middle schools reported that they used them. This is surprising as it was expected that home visits would be used more often with children in middle schools, since they are younger than those at secondary school. This difference may be at least partly due to the fact that secondary schools in New Zealand have guidance counselors available to make home visits, whereas middle schools do not. However, it does highlight the possible underuse of one aspect of parental involvement in middle schools, which many parents appreciate, especially parents of children with special educational or medical needs. (see Chap. 6 for guidelines on the use of home visits).

Case Studies of English and Barbadian Secondary Schools

In order to gain some degree of international comparison, interviews were conducted at two secondary schools, one in England and one in Barbados, using the same interview schedule used in the New Zealand studies. The students at both schools were aged from 11 to 18 years, as in both countries children typically move directly from elementary to secondary schools, as middle schools are uncommon. The English school had a roll of 1,300 students, and the Barbadian school had a roll of 1,069 students. Both schools were selective in their intake and catered mainly for students with high levels of academic ability. Both of the interviewees, the deputy principal in England and the principal in Barbados, were very experienced educators known to the author. However, whereas the English school operated in an education system that strongly encourages and expects high levels of parent involvement, the Barbadian education system is a much more traditional one, in which home–school collaboration is not expected by either parents or teachers. Findings from the interviews are summarized below.

English Secondary School

Policy Formation

The school has no overall written policy for parental involvement, but there are policies on "communication with parents" and "home–school agreements." There is a PTA but with only around 20 regular members. The school does not have a room set aside for parents' use. Parents' views about school policies or procedures are occasionally sought via questionnaires or focus groups. New members for the school's Board of Governors are recruited through letters sent to all parents.

Acting as a Resource

Parents are informed about ways they could help at school through regular newsletters and a "new parents" handbook. Volunteer help from parents is mainly with sports teams, clubs, and outdoor activities. Parent volunteers are organized by the individual teachers involved.

Collaborating with Teachers

Students' grades are sent home to parents every 6 weeks and in annual formal reports. Parent–teacher meetings are held once a year. Parent support of school programs is through an expectation that parents check up on homework and monitor children when put "on report" for behavioral issues or poor progress.

Sharing Information on Children

Information on children's special or medical needs is obtained from enrolment forms and previous schools as well as when new parents meet with form tutors, heads of year, the SEN coordinator, or the school nurse. This information is disseminated to teachers at a staff meeting at the start of the year. Parents are asked to update this information annually or as necessary, and updated information is e-mailed directly to teachers.

Channels of Communication

Parents are kept informed about what is happening at school through the twice-termly newsletters, through the school website and letters home and through text messaging. A parent handbook is used to inform parents of their rights and responsibilities. For years seven through nine (US grades eight through ten), letters are sent to parents to acknowledge commendations achieved by students. Parents are expected to phone, write notes, e-mail, or make appointments to see form tutors or heads of year if they have concerns, though if parents arrive without prior notice, every effort is made to set up a meeting.

Liaison with School Staff

Parent–teacher meetings are held yearly, additionally, "reports evenings" are set up for parents to be able to talk with heads of year if children's reports have raised any issues. Also, heads of year may make home visits when there is a problem. Home–school diaries are used with all students and focus mainly on homework completion.

Parent Education

Parents can observe teaching in progress on "open days." Teachers can provide guidance to parents at parent–teacher meetings. Parents are informed about parent education courses via a booklet on evening classes offered at the school. Workshops for parents are organized when required, such as the recent ones on "misuse of the internet" and "dealing with adolescents."

Parent Support

Parents can discuss their concerns with teachers at annual parent–teacher meetings or at specially organized meetings when needed and are referred on to community agencies that provide counselling and guidance when necessary.

Encouraging Parents into School

The school uses open days, new parents evenings, school performances, exhibitions of pupils' work, and talks by invited speakers to encourage parents to come to school. The first meeting for new parents has a social aspect, with wine and cheese, to facilitate parents meeting each other and form tutors. There is also an annual grandparents' day and access to the school website for parents.

Involving Diverse Parents

The school admissions booklet is produced in three languages, and help is offered to families for whom English is not their first language. When necessary sign language interpreters are brought in to help family members who are deaf. Parents participate fully in reviews of IEPs, by providing written advice beforehand, attending meetings, and contributing to the setting of targets for the subsequent year.

Professional Development for Teachers

Recently qualified teachers at the school have had training on communicating with parents as part of their initial teacher training. Also, advice is given to newly qualified teachers in preparation for annual parent–teacher meetings. Occasionally, parents of children with SEN, such as visual impairment and Asperger's syndrome, have participated in in-service training for teachers.

Barbadian Secondary School

Policy Formation

The school does not have a written policy for parental involvement but does have an active PTA. The PTA meets monthly on Saturdays and attracts 150–200 parents. Fund-raising by the PTA raises substantial sums of money for the school. PTA members are recruited through letters sent to new parents. Parents are able to use the school's boardroom for meetings.

Acting as a Resource

Parents are informed about ways they can help at school through PTA meetings and newsletters. Parents help with the annual fair and with sports and other activities after school.

Collaborating with Teachers

Assessments of children are communicated to parents at parent–teacher meetings and through school reports. Reports on academic progress are sent home to parents at the end of each half-term and in annual formal reports. Parents' support of school programs is through an expectation that parents check the school's online homework site and supervise their children in completing homework.

Sharing Information on Children

Information on children's special needs is obtained at enrolment and is disseminated to teachers via memos from the principal or deputy principal. Parents' insights on their children are reported to be welcomed but are not solicited.

Channels of Communication

A parent handbook is used to inform parents of their rights and responsibilities. Parents with concerns can just drop in to school, phone, or write notes, or make appointments to see teachers. They are also able to speak with the year head or principal as necessary. The principal encourages teachers to be proactive and inform parents when students are performing well.

Liaison with School Staff

The school guidance counsellor makes home visits when necessary, but teachers do not. Home–school diaries are used only for students with severe behavior problems.

Parent Education

Parents can observe teaching in progress on "open days." Teachers arrange for parents to visit the school for guidance, when requested. Parents are made aware of parent education workshops offered by government agencies.

Parent Support

Parents can discuss their concerns with other parents at monthly PTA meetings. The principal refers parents to community agencies that provide counseling and guidance when necessary.

Encouraging Parents into School

The school uses open days, new parents evenings, exhibitions of pupils' work, and school fairs to encourage parents to come into the school. It operates an "open-door" policy to accommodate parents who drop in without an appointment.

Involving Diverse Parents

The school has few students for whom English is not the first language and has no students on IEPs. Parents of gifted children are encouraged to place them in after-school programs.

Professional Development for Teachers

Teachers may have had training on working with parents as part of their initial teacher education, or as part of teacher in-service training days, but this is not certain.

Comparison of Parental Involvement in English and Barbadian Schools

The case studies of these English and Barbadian secondary schools highlight similar variability in policy and practices of parental involvement to those that were found in the New Zealand middle and secondary schools reported on earlier in this chapter. However, there were differences between the two schools in their provision of parental involvement. For example, the English school used a wider range of mechanisms for communicating and collaborating with parents. The Barbadian school had a greater involvement of parents in the PTA, albeit that their role was mainly restricted to fund-raising. Similarities included neither school seeming to place much emphasis on the provision of parent education, which is essential if parents are to fully realize the key role they can play at home in supporting their children's education. This is particularly important at the Barbadian school, which is operating in a societal culture that does not emphasize parental involvement in children's education.

Summary and Conclusion

This chapter reports the results of surveys of parental involvement practices at middle and secondary schools in New Zealand, as well as case studies of parental involvement at secondary schools in England and Barbados. Similar to the findings of the survey of elementary schools reported in the previous chapter, notable gaps in provision for parental involvement in the middle and secondary schools surveyed were as follows: a lack of written school policies for parental involvement, the ad hoc nature of the organization of parental involvement by schools, minimal use of home visits, the lack of specific strategies to involve diverse parents, a limited focus on parent education, and a lack of training for teachers on parental involvement. Guidelines for implementing the major parental involvement practices identified in this chapter as needing more consistent implementation across schools are discussed in Chap. 6.

Chapter 6
Guidelines for Implementing Parent Involvement Activities

Introduction

The types of parental involvement found to be most engaged in by the schools surveyed were as follows: various informal activities for encouraging parents to come to school, varied formats of parent–teacher meetings, both formal and informal, a variety of forms of written communication, telephone contacts and to a lesser extent use of new technological options, and home visits. Guidelines for professionals such as psychologists, school counselors, and teachers for effectively implementing these various forms of parental involvement are presented in this chapter. These guidelines are based on the author's experience as an educational psychologist, teacher, and teacher educator, as well as on the now extensive literature on implementing effective strategies for parental involvement (Grant & Ray, 2010; Henderson, Mapp, Johnson, & Davies, 2007; Kroth, 1985; Seligman, 2000; Simpson, 1996; Swap, 1993; Turnbull, Turnbull, Erwin, Soodak, & Shogren, 2011).

Activities for Encouraging Parents into School

The schools surveyed all used various informal activities to encourage parents to get involved with the school. Informal contacts are a useful way of "breaking the ice" in most forms of human relationships, and this is also the case in relationships with parents. Such contacts provide a means whereby parents and school staff can meet each other as people with a mutual interest in building relationships on behalf of children, thereby helping to break down the barriers that often exist between school and home. Informal contacts are particularly important for parents of children newly enrolled at the school or when there has not been a high level of parent involvement at the school in the past. In the latter situation, teachers understandably become despondent when the attendance at more formal events, such as parents' evenings, is so poor. When this is the case, it is often best to organize informal events to increase the numbers of parents having contact with the school and thereby establish the context necessary for the development of other forms of contact.

G. Hornby, *Parental Involvement in Childhood Education: Building Effective School-Family Partnerships*, DOI 10.1007/978-1-4419-8379-4_6,
© Springer Science+Business Media, LLC 2011

The organization of informal contacts is illustrated by the following descriptions of four different types of activities: school productions, open days, gala days, and outings to the local community.

Organization of Informal Events

School Productions

The type of informal occasion guaranteed to achieve the maximum attendance of parents is one in which they see their children perform in some way or other. It is often possible to organize activities so that a large proportion of children attending the school are involved in such events as school concerts or nativity plays and thereby ensure excellent attendance of parents.

Open Days

Another way to encourage a large proportion of parents to come to the school is to have an "open day" or "open evening" when parents can come along to look around the school and see classes in progress, along with displays of their children's work.

Outings

Class or year-group or even school outings to places such as local parks on weekends or at holiday times can attract large numbers of parents and other family members.

Gala Days or School Fairs

Events whose main aim is raising funds for the school, by having stalls that sell homemade food and activities such as races for children and adults, also provide opportunities for teachers, parents, and children to meet informally.

Ensuring Success of Informal Events

Karther and Lowden (1997) suggest that "Events at the school will draw more families if they are of an informal tone; if food, child-care, and, if necessary, transportation are provided; and if the students participate in some way for or with their parents" (p. 43). Other suggestions for making informal occasions successful are outlined below.

Personal Invitations

In addition to the event being advertised in the school newsletter, parents should receive individually addressed invitations, possibly produced and delivered by their children. Invitations should give at least 2 weeks notice of the event so that parents can make the necessary arrangements. Then, 2 or 3 days before the event, reminder notes should be sent home with their children.

Facilitating Attendance

The two major difficulties that many parents experience in arranging to attend school events are with transportation and child care. Providing assistance in each of these areas will improve attendance rates. For example, organizing car pools or minibuses to pick up parents will enable some parents to come who otherwise would not have been able to. Also, organizing child-care facilities or making the event suitable for the whole family to attend is likely to substantially increase attendance. Finally, it is worth bearing in mind that events planned for evenings and weekends are more likely to get fathers involved.

Welcoming Atmosphere

The first step taken in any form of parental involvement should be to make parents feel welcome. For events held at the school, it is important to make the school entrance and foyer as welcoming as possible. Ideally, when parents first arrive, they should be greeted and shown around by children or other parents. If this is not possible, then directions to where the event is to be held should be clearly signposted.

Optimizing Opportunities for Informal Communication

Careful planning is required to ensure that informal events do provide opportunities for parents and teachers to mix and talk with each other. Seating arrangements and planned activities should be organized to facilitate mixing rather than allowing people to sit with others they already know.

Providing Food and Drink

One of the best ways of promoting informal conversation is through arranging for food and drink at an event. There is something about eating and drinking with other people that helps to cement relationships and build rapport. Potluck meals, where everyone brings a plate of home-cooked food, are particularly good for this.

Evaluating Activities

Inviting parents to formally and informally evaluate activities ensures that their feedback can be used to improve future events.

Parent–Teacher Meetings

The form of contact that all the schools that were surveyed reported using is that of parent–teacher interviews or meetings. These meetings are an established method of involving parents and not without reason, as research has shown that they have an impact on both parent–teacher relationships and pupil progress (Turnbull & Turnbull, 1986). It has been found that children whose parents attend such meetings have higher attendance rates, fewer behavior problems, and improved academic achievement. Of course, experienced teachers would immediately suggest that this is because the parents of "good kids" usually attend parents' evenings, whereas parents of pupils with behavioral or learning difficulties tend not to turn up. However, as noted in Chap. 2, it must not be assumed that parents who do not turn up to parents' evenings are not interested in their children's education. There is a variety of reasons why some parents do not attend such meetings, including transport and babysitting problems, as well as parents' negative feelings about their own school days. Perhaps if these problems could be overcome, then these parents would come to parents' evenings and this would lead to better parent–teacher relationships and thereby an improvement in their children's behavior and progress at school. However, it is usually easier to use other strategies to communicate with these parents than to overcome these problems. By using either telephone contacts or home visits or written communication, good parent–teacher relationships can be established, which will lead to improvements in children's behavior and academic progress.

It is typically only a minority of parents who do not come to parents' evenings. Regular parent–teacher meetings are desired by the majority of parents. The fact that nearly all schools hold such meetings suggests that teachers also find that they are a useful way of communicating between home and school. However, Bastiani (1989) has suggested that teachers and parents have different goals for such meetings. These are identified below.

Goals for Parent–Teacher Meetings

Teachers' Goals

- Informing parents of their children's progress
- Establishing good relationships with parents
- Telling parents about the difficulties their children have at school
- Checking with parents how their children are coping with school
- Learning more about children, from parents' perspectives

- Finding out parents' opinions about the school program
- Identifying ways in which parents can help their children at home
- Identifying potential conflicts between parents and teachers
- Jointly making decisions about children's education

Parents' Goals

- Meeting all the people who teach their children
- Finding out about their children's progress
- Finding out about any difficulties they are having
- Passing on important information about their children
- Questioning teachers about any concerns they have
- Finding out ways of helping their children at home
- Comparing their children's progress with that of others in the class
- Discussing any difficulties that they are experiencing at home
- Learning more about the school and the methods of teaching used

In addition, Swap (1993) has suggested that an important hidden agenda that parents have at such meetings is to check whether the teacher really knows and understands their child.

Whatever goals teachers and parents have for these meetings, it is important to both participants that they are organized to ensure effective communication. Several authors have provided suggestions for optimizing the effectiveness of parent–teacher meetings (Grant & Ray, 2010; Kroth, 1985; Seligman, 2000; Simpson, 1996; Swap, 1993; Turnbull et al., 2011). It is from these sources that the following guidelines are drawn. The guidelines are divided into three sections focusing on tasks for before and after meetings and those for actually conducting meetings.

Organization of Parent–Teacher Meetings

Because of the typically large number of parents each teacher has to meet with, there is considerable time pressure on parent–teacher interviews. It is therefore important to do as much as possible beforehand to ensure that time in the meeting is used as effectively as possible. The following guidelines are suggested with this aim in mind and will also apply to additional parent–teacher interviews that are set up at the request of either parents or teachers.

Making Initial Contacts

It is of course preferable if the teacher's first contact with parents is not in a formal parent–teacher interview. It is far better if the initial contact is made by means of one of the informal forms of contact discussed earlier. However, this is not always possible, so for many parents this formal situation will be their first contact with their children's teachers.

Notifying Parents

Notifying parents about parent–teacher meetings is usually best done by letters of invitation sent home at least 2 weeks in advance, if possible followed up by less formal reminders 2 or 3 days beforehand. Reminders can be a brief note in a child's school bag or a short telephone call. Invitations need to specify the place, time, and duration of the meeting. The purpose of the meeting should be made quite clear and nonthreatening so that parents do not worry unnecessarily. Many secondary schools in New Zealand now use software on the school Web site that enables parents to book interview times that suit them a few days beforehand. This makes the process more efficient for parents and teachers.

Helping Parents Prepare

Along with the invitation, parents can be sent some guidelines to help them prepare for the meeting. Kroth (1985) suggests that most parents appreciate this because it conveys a message that parental input is welcome at the meeting. Guidelines for parents should include the following:

- Making a list of questions to ask or concerns to raise. For example, about the child's progress in various subjects, behavior in class and the playground, relationships with teachers and other children
- Being prepared to ask for clarification of any unfamiliar terms or other aspects of the child's program, which the teacher refers to
- Being prepared to comment on children's activities at home, such as hobbies or interests
- Being prepared to comment on the way children behave at home and what limits are set, for example, regarding TV viewing, homework completion, and bedtime
- Being prepared to comment on factors that may affect children's learning, such as child's health, or that of other family members, or any other relevant family circumstances
- Talking to children beforehand to check whether they have any concerns or questions they would like the teacher to be asked

Preparing Room

Since the physical environment has an impact on the quality of communication in meetings, it is important to arrange for the most suitable venue available. Typically, at elementary schools, the teacher's classroom will be used, and this need not be inappropriate as long as certain basic steps are taken. For example, the most comfortable chairs available should be found and arranged so that there are no physical barriers, such as a desks, between parents and the teacher. Also, distractions should be avoided and privacy maintained by keeping the classroom door closed and having a "Do Not Disturb" sign on the outside of it. Secondary schools typically use the school hall for parent–teacher meetings, so there is usually a lot of noise and no privacy; therefore, if serious issues need to be discussed, it is better to arrange a meeting with parents another time.

Reviewing Children's Work and Grades

Before the meeting, it is useful to review children's records, assessment data, grades, and work done at school. Typical examples of children's work can be selected to show parents at the meeting.

Involving Other Staff

Where relevant, it is also important to talk with other members of staff who work with the children, such as the dean or school counselor, to obtain more information and get their views on the children's progress.

Preparing Agenda

A list of issues needing to be raised with parents should be made and these should be ranked in order of priority so that key concerns can be dealt with first. It may not be possible to cover all of the issues, since parents are likely to want time to discuss items of concern to them.

Involving Children

Around a third of the New Zealand elementary schools surveyed reported involving children in meetings along with their parents. This approach has come to be known as *student-led parent–teacher meetings* (Little & Allan, 1989). In student-led meetings, children typically introduce their parents to their teacher and show selected samples of their work to parents. Teachers then present data on children's achievements, strengths, and weaknesses. Then, parents, teachers, and children work together to set goals for children to work on. One principal of a middle school in the USA reports that implementing this approach has increased participation of parents from 45 to 95% (Kinney, 2005). She suggests that other benefits of student-led conferences include parents gaining a clearer understanding of expectations for learning, and children learning skills in goal-setting, self-reflection, and communication, as well as facilitating the involvement of parents for whom English is a second language. Therefore, involving children in parent–teacher meetings in this way is an important approach for schools to consider.

Conducting Parent–Teacher Meetings

Although the focus of meetings is necessarily on the issues to be discussed, it must not be forgotten that establishing effective working relationships with parents is more important in the long term. So, the manner in which meetings are conducted is of vital importance. It has been suggested that, in the past, parent–teacher meetings have been characterized by a one-way flow of information, from teacher to parent (Simpson, 1996). However, as noted earlier, relationships between parents and teachers can only be successful if there is a two-way communication process that involves sharing information, concerns, and ideas. Therefore, to conduct effective meetings with parents, teachers need to use many of the interpersonal skills that are discussed in Chap. 7, plus those that are referred to below.

Rapport Building

When parents first arrive, time should be spent welcoming them and making them feel at ease. They should be thanked for coming and encouraged to ask questions or comment at any time during the meeting.

Structuring

It is always wise to remind parents of the time limits set for the meeting, since there is good evidence that setting time limits helps to reduce irrelevant discussion (Simpson, 1996). Then, the purpose of the meeting can be stated, and the agenda items proposed by the teacher can be listed. Parents should be asked if there are other issues or concerns they would like to discuss at the meeting. Parents' items can then be added to the agenda, which should then be dealt with in an agreed priority order.

Note-Taking

It is easier to build a rapport in a meeting if notes are not taken during it. However, teachers often find it useful to note important details and list things they need to do after the meeting. Parents may also want to make notes. So, the issue of note-taking should be discussed at the beginning of the meeting. If teachers explain the reasons for wanting to take notes, are sensitive about what they write down, and are willing to allow parents see what they have written, then this should not interfere with the communication process.

Providing Information

It is usually best to start on a positive note by stating the areas in which the child is doing well. Concerns the teacher has about difficulties the child is experiencing or creating should be stated clearly and specifically but with sensitivity. Parents want teachers to be honest with them but not brutal. If part of the difficulty that teachers need to convey involves providing some negative feedback to parents, for example, if pupils are consistently not doing their homework and parents do not appear to be monitoring this, then the modified DESC script (see Chap. 7) can be used.

Obtaining Information

In order to get parents to open up and share concerns and ideas, teachers need to use the skills of attentiveness, asking open-ended questions, paraphrasing, and using active listening, the details of which are discussed in Chap. 7.

Problem-Solving

Where specific problems emerge with no obvious solutions or where teachers and parents disagree, then the problem-solving procedure, which is discussed in Chap. 7, should be used.

Termination

At the end of the meeting, teachers should summarize the main points that have emerged and review the action that both parents and teachers have agreed to take. If more time is needed, then further meetings should be arranged. Finally, parents should be thanked for their participation and reminded that they can contact the school any time they require information or have a concern about their child.

Reviewing Parent–Teacher Meetings

Following the meeting, teachers have several tasks to complete to make best use of the outcome of the meeting. These are outlined below.

Making a Record

A brief report should be written to summarize the main issues that were discussed and the decisions that emerged from the meeting. It should record the individuals responsible for carrying out each recommendation that was agreed upon.

Discuss with Children

A brief review of the items discussed at the meeting should be conducted with the children involved and the impact of any recommendations on them explained to them. Children should then be given the opportunity to ask questions about the meeting.

Liaise with Colleagues

Other members of staff should be informed about the outcome of the meeting and any recommendations relevant to their work with the child discussed with them.

Plan for Follow-Up

Teachers need to plan for the implementation of the recommendations agreed at the meeting and for any follow-up meetings that were scheduled.

Evaluate

One way for teachers to get feedback from parents on the effectiveness of the meetings from their perspective is to ask parents to complete a brief questionnaire on which they are asked to rate aspects of the parent–teacher meeting, such as the suitability of the room used, the adequacy of the time available, the appropriateness of the agenda, the adequacy of information obtained, the quality of the teacher's listening skills, and the helpfulness of the recommendations made.

Written Communication

Research findings reported in Chaps. 4 and 5 indicated that various forms of written communication were used by schools to inform and communicate with parents. The most commonly used were newsletters, handbooks, and progress reports, although letters or notes, and home–school diaries or notebooks were also widely used. It is therefore clear that the written word provides an important means of communication between teachers and parents (Grant & Ray, 2010; Turnbull et al., 2011).

However, there are two major difficulties with this form of communication. First, if some of the pupils' parents do not have English as their first language, then ideally every written communication to parents needs to be translated into their own languages. Second, it is important to remember that some parents have reading difficulties themselves. Therefore, written materials cannot be relied upon to communicate effectively with all parents. This suggests that all written materials should use language that is simple and able to be understood by the majority of parents.

Handbooks

Most of the schools surveyed had parent handbooks or school prospectuses, the purpose of which is to inform new or prospective parents about the school's aims and organization. These tend to be general documents that focus on promoting positive features of the school and informing parents about the major school rules and policies for pupils and parents to be aware of. It has been suggested by Kroth (1985) that parents of children with special educational needs (SEN) appreciate having a handbook written especially for them, but none of the schools surveyed mentioned having this. Parent handbooks should inform parents about their rights and responsibilities regarding their children, along with all the information they need to help them to be happy and successful at the school. Parent handbooks or prospectuses should address the following aspects of school life.

Personnel

School staff, such as deans or heads of year, and the school's coordinator for SEN, should be listed along with their contact phone numbers, as well as those of specialists such as school psychologists and counselors.

Policies

The school's policy for parental involvement and for meeting children's SEN should be clearly spelled out. These should include an explanation for parents of who to contact if they have a concern and of the best methods for making this contact.

School-Wide Procedures

School rules regarding dress and discipline should be briefly outlined and the specific procedures for rewarding effort and progress, as well as for dealing with misbehavior should be explained.

Classroom Procedures

An indication of the materials and equipment children will need for various subjects should be included, as well as suggestions for where these can be obtained.

Transport

The arrangements for transporting children to and from school should be detailed.

Reports Home

A description of the type and frequency of the progress reports parents will receive should be included.

Other information

Any other information that would be helpful to parents should be included, such as details of parent education workshops that are based at the school.

Newsletters

Newsletters regularly sent out to parents, typically once or twice a term, are a very good way of communicating with the majority of parents. Newsletters can be general ones that are addressed to all parents of children at the school, or more specific ones addressed to parents of children in a particular year, or just to the parents of children who are gifted or those with SEN. Newsletters can include a variety of content including notices for forthcoming events, updates of ongoing school projects, and invitations for parents to provide voluntary help at the school.

Letters and Notes

Letters are a time-consuming and formal means for communicating with parents. Therefore, it is generally better to use the other forms of communication described above for most purposes and only use letters for situations that require a more formal approach. For example, most schools will, as a last resort, use letters to express concern about a child's behavior and invite parents to come to school to discuss the problem. However, this use of letters to deal with discipline problems should be balanced by a system of positive letters sent to parents to acknowledge a child's outstanding effort or progress, as was done at some of the schools surveyed.

In contrast to formal letters, teachers often find it useful to send brief handwritten notes home to parents via children's school bags. This can be a quick and effective way of getting a message to parents who teachers already have a good relationship with, but it does have its drawbacks. Notes can sometimes become lost on the way home or can be overlooked. Also, there is no record kept of what has been written.

Home–School Diaries

Many parents prefer to have some form of book for written communication between themselves and teachers. These were used at several of the schools surveyed for certain children, such as those with SEN, while at some schools they were used for all children. It is more difficult for a book to be overlooked or lost, it provides a record of messages sent home, and it allows parents to write a message back to the teacher if they wish so. However, some parents are reluctant to write notes back to the teacher because they do not want to expose their weaknesses in spelling or grammar.

Others may think that they have little of value to write back to the teacher about. So, teachers should accept that although they encourage all parents to reply to their comments in home–school diaries, parents will vary in their use of this opportunity. Simply because parents do not write in the diary does not mean that they do not value it.

The home–school diary can be used to exchange information with parents on a wide variety of subjects. For example, it can be used to let parents know about children's accomplishments at school. Or a note can be made of the topics discussed and activities carried out by children at school so that these can be discussed by parents at home. Alternatively, what children have done at home during the evening or the weekend or the holidays can be noted so that the teacher can follow up these topics at school. Similarly, parents can inform teachers about any circumstances at home that may have upset their child, while teachers can let parents know about any misbehavior that has occurred at school. However, it is best not to communicate essentially sensitive or negative information by means of the diary. This is better done face-to-face, as mentioned earlier.

Turnbull and Turnbull (1986) suggest that parents should be involved in deciding what information is included in the diary as well as how often it will be sent home and whether parents want to write in it. When parents do write in the diary this method of communication generally works very well and makes a significant contribution to strengthening relationships between the parents and teachers concerned.

Weekly Folder

This is a variation on the home–school diary, suggested by Sicley (1993). It is simply an A4 size folder with a sheet of paper with a line down the middle stapled inside it. At the end of the week, the teacher writes a brief message for parents on the left-hand side of the sheet and encloses in the folder notices, newsletters, details of homework, or samples of the childrens' work for their parents to see. When the folder is taken home, parents then have the opportunity to write a comment on the sheet next to the teacher's message. When the sheets get filled up, new ones are stapled on top of the old ones so that a record of the messages can be kept. In this way, the weekly folder provides a quick and efficient method for maintaining contact with parents and keeping them in touch with what their children are doing at school.

Progress Reports

Reports on children's progress are the most longstanding and widely used form of written communication to parents and are a legal requirement in most school systems. All schools surveyed used some form of progress reports, but there was wide variation in how many reports were sent to parents each school year. There was also variation in the formats of such reports with some schools organizing these around portfolios of children's work that were sent home for parents to see. Formats for reporting to parents have been undergoing changes in many countries in recent years. One type of report that has been popular with schools in England is the *Record of Achievement*. Although each school develops its own format, records of achievement have several common components. First, they list the major achievements made by the pupil in each subject area. Second, pupils comment on these achievements and on their satisfaction with their progress in each subject and on any specific weaknesses they have. Third, pupils state their immediate goals in each subject. Fourth, teachers comment on pupils' achievements and on their immediate goals. Then, reports based on this process are sent out to parents, typically once a year.

Our own children attended elementary schools in three countries, England, Barbados, and New Zealand so, as parents, we have experienced a wide variety of types of progress reports. Formats of reports have also varied as they went from elementary, through middle, to secondary school in New Zealand. From a parent's perspective, many of these reports have not been all that useful in that they have been difficult to interpret and lacked clear information about progress and future needs. Since teachers spend a lot of time writing these reports, it is important for schools to check that they provide the information that parents want and do this in a clear way that is understandable to people who are not in the education profession. One way to get useful feedback from parents on the format of progress reports is to organize focus groups with parents from varied backgrounds. The middle school that my sons attended did this one year and found the feedback to be very useful in revising the format of their reporting procedure, which was subsequently found to be more time-efficient for teachers and more appreciated by parents.

Telephone Contacts

Telephone contacts were reported to be used by many of the schools surveyed, but by no means all of them. Nowadays, the vast majority of parents have a telephone. So most parents are quite comfortable about communicating with teachers by means of the telephone, and many parents prefer to maintain contact with teachers in this way (Turnbull et al., 2011).

Parents Phoning Teachers

Many parents appreciate the opportunity of being able to phone teachers directly either at school or at home. However, there are difficulties associated with both of these options. The main problem with parents phoning teachers at school is that teachers should only have to leave their class to answer the telephone in absolute emergencies. So it is usually best to get the school secretary take messages and tell parents that the teacher will phone back as soon as possible.

Many teachers are not prepared to allow parents to phone them at home. This is perfectly understandable, since they may feel the need to have some time to themselves, or with their own families, which work pressures do not impinge on. Other teachers may want to encourage parents to phone them at home in preference to being phoned at school. An alternative solution is to set a specified time of day or evening during the week when parents know the teacher will be at home and available to answer the phone.

Teachers Phoning Parents

Teachers should check whether some parents are at home during the day and others are happy to be phoned at work, in which case at least some of the calls could be made from school during the day. Otherwise, it means phoning parents in the evening in teachers' own time.

Whenever telephone calls are made to parents, there are certain guidelines that it is wise to follow. The following guidelines were adapted from the suggestions made by Turnbull and Turnbull (1986).

1. Identify yourself as their child's teacher when parents first answer.
2. Ask if it is a convenient time to talk or whether it would be better if you called back later.
3. Make a point of finding out the best time to call parents. Usually, later in the evening, when children are in bed, is the most suitable time.
4. Use a written list of things you want to ask or tell parents that you have prepared beforehand.
5. Be concise and to the point. If an issue needs lengthy discussion, it is better to do it face-to-face than over the phone.
6. Listen carefully to what the parent has to say, using the listening skills discussed in Chap. 7.
7. Give the parent time to ask you questions and to think about the things you have said.
8. If you do not have the information that parents want, suggest that you will find out and get back to them as soon as possible.
9. Avoid relaying sensitive information over telephone. This is better done face-to-face so that parents' reactions can be gauged.
10. Always finish by thanking parents for their time and remind them that they can contact you anytime they have a concern.

Other Uses of the Telephone

Two other uses of the telephone in working with parents are suggested by Turnbull and Turnbull (1986). First, a *telephone tree* can be used as an efficient way to get information to parents. Once the list (or tree) of parents' names and phone numbers is circulated to all parents, the teacher simply has to ring the first name on the list and parents then ring each other in turn to pass on the information. Variations on this system include the teacher phoning two parents who in turn phone another two parents. This continues until all parents have been contacted. An additional benefit of the telephone tree is that parents are encouraged to interact with one another, which may lead to supportive friendships being formed.

Second, an answer phone can be used to play *recorded daily messages* for parents who ring the school phone number in the evening or at the weekend. For example, messages can be recorded to tell parents about the activities the class have been involved in during the day, about the homework that has been set or to remind them about the equipment needed for the following day. Turnbull and Turnbull (1986) report a study that found that children performed better on homework tasks using the system of recorded daily messages rather than the traditional homework diaries.

New Technological Options for Communication

Use of new communication options such as e-mail and school websites were mentioned by several schools but not by the vast majority of schools. It is considered that such strategies have great potential for increasing effective parental involvement and, along with other recent innovations, will become an integral part of schools' strategies for parental involvement in the future (Howe & Simmons, 2005; Turnbull et al., 2011). Therefore, guidelines for using new communication options for improving parental involvement are outlined below.

Websites

School websites have so far been used mainly to provide information about the school for parents and others to access. Simply by providing information about which staff to contact about various issues and their e-mail addresses can be useful for parents. Class websites are less common but have great potential for strengthening home–school links (Grant & Ray, 2010). They can be used as a learning tool for children as well as a means of communication with parents. For example, putting information about homework assignments on the class website provides guidelines for children but also lets parents know what is expected, so they can support their children in completing homework. The website can also be used to present details of forthcoming activities and photographs of class activities and trips. In addition, the website can be used to display ideas for home activities for parents to engage in with children to support their learning.

E-mail

A few of the schools surveyed were beginning to use e-mail to communicate with parents. School and class newsletters can be sent out by e-mail, saving printing and mailing costs, and avoiding newsletters being "lost" at the bottom of school bags. Schools should ask parents to opt in to having newsletters e-mailed out so that the minority of families without the internet can be sent print copies. E-mail is also very useful for schools checking on children's absences.

Text Messaging

Since most families will have at least one cellular or mobile phone, this provides a potential means of contacting parents urgently if this is necessary, as in the case of sickness or an injury to their child. It is also a useful means of checking on school absences.

Blogging

Blogging, which is basically online journaling, is a very recent development and was not mentioned by any of the schools surveyed. However, it is considered that it has great potential for facilitating parental involvement (Turnbull et al., 2011). It is possible for classroom teachers to post blogs on the internet at the end of every school day highlighting class activities, thereby enabling parents to share in their children's experiences and support their children's learning at home. A variety of material can be posted on blogs – text, photographs, and video clips, which make it a very flexible medium. Teachers will need to be cautious though about violating children's privacy, as blogs can be read by anyone with access to the internet.

Home Visits

Rationale for Making Home Visits

Home visits were reported to be used by a minority of schools. However, since many parents appreciate it when their children's teachers are prepared to come and visit them on their own territory, such home visits can be pivotal in establishing constructive working relationships with parents (Grant & Ray, 2010). They provide teachers with an opportunity to see for themselves the circumstances in which the family is living.

They also enable teachers to meet other members of the family such as siblings, fathers, and grandparents who they may not otherwise meet. Knowledge of these factors can help teachers understand how their pupils may be affected by the home situation. Most importantly, home visits provide an ideal opportunity for teachers to answer parents' questions and deal with any concerns they may have. In addition, home visits enable teachers to find out how their pupils spend their time at home, whether they have any hobbies, how much television they watch, and what time they usually go to bed. It is also possible to find out how pupils behave at home and how their parents manage their behavior.

However, not all parents want home visits. Some parents may be too embarrassed to allow teachers to see their homes, others may fear what neighbors may say about a teacher's visit. Also, as found in the surveys reported in Chaps. 4 and 5, most schools do not see home visits as a high priority, for several reasons. First, schools are generally not aware of just how much many parents appreciate receiving home visits. Second, schools may not realize the benefits that can accrue for teachers and children from making such home visits. Third, home visits are very time-consuming and often need to be carried out in the evening, which for teachers with their own families is not easy. Fourth, there are issues of personal safety, especially for young female teachers making home visits in some of the communities in which the families of the children that they teach are living. Fifth, many teachers, especially inexperienced ones, are diffident about relating to parents, so home visits are daunting for them. Following the guidelines below should make them less so.

Guidelines for Making Home Visits

In order to optimize the effectiveness of home visits some general guidelines should be followed. These are outlined below.

Arranging Visits

Home visits should always be prearranged, since some parents would be embarrassed about the tidiness and cleanliness of their home if teachers just arrived unannounced. It is usually best for teachers to write letters to parents saying that they wish to make home visits to the parents of all their pupils and will be phoning in the next few days to make arrangements with those parents who would like this.

Dress

Since in their own homes parents will be dressed casually, it is best if teachers dress less formally than they do at school so that parents will feel more at ease. Some parents may find it more difficult to open up with a teacher dressed formally when they are dressed casually.

Time

It is clearly best to arrange to visit at a time of day when all the family members will be present and when parents will have a chance to talk. For most families, the middle of the evening, when families have finished their evening meal, is the best time. It is important to be punctual and to allow sufficient time for the visit. It is also important not to stay too long as parents will need time to get the children ready for bed and possibly do other chores and get ready for the morning. It is usually best to allow for visits to last for around an hour but to set a time limit 15 min before your actual deadline to cope with the phenomenon that parents will mention their greatest concern just as you are leaving.

Courtesy

It is important to respect the hospitality associated with the cultural group from which the family comes. With most English families, this will simply mean accepting the offer of a cup of tea or coffee, but for West Indian families it will probably mean accepting something to eat as well. When I was teaching in New Zealand and made a home visit to a Samoan family, I found that they had prepared a full meal of Samoan food all served on banana leaves for my arrival. Fortunately, I had been forewarned that it is not possible to discuss important matters in a Samoan household until you have shared food with the family.

Listening

Throughout the visit, teachers need to be aware of using the listening skills discussed in Chap. 7 to help parents express their priorities and concerns about their children.

Questions

Teachers will want to ask parents for information about their children such as about any medical problems or about their behavior at home. It is also important to allow parents time to ask questions of the teacher.

Distractions

Teachers should anticipate that there are likely to be distractions, such as parents needing to answer the telephone, during the visit and be determined not to become irritated by them.

Summary and Conclusion

A range of strategies used by schools for communicating with parents have been discussed in this chapter. Informal contacts such as open days, school productions, and outings were suggested as ways of "breaking the ice." Several forms of written communication have been considered including handbooks, newsletters, progress reports, and home–school diaries. Guidelines have also been provided for the use of telephone contacts with parents, and for the use of new technological options such as school websites, e-mail, and text messaging. In addition, the organization, conduct, and review of parent–teacher meetings have been discussed at length. Finally, the importance of home visits in building relationships with parents was stressed and guidelines for making them were provided.

In conclusion, it can be seen that a wide variety of strategies can be used for communicating with parents. The actual strategies used by schools should respond to parent preferences. Therefore, it is considered that making a range of strategies available to parents will lead to optimal levels of parental involvement in schools. However, the range of strategies used by schools will mostly be dependent on teachers' knowledge of and skills for effectively implementing the various strategies. The skills required by teachers for implementing a wide range of activities and strategies for parental involvement are presented in Chap. 7.

Chapter 7
Skills for Effective Parent Involvement

Introduction

In order to work effectively with parents, professionals such as teachers, psychologists, social workers, and counselors working in schools need to have good interpersonal communication skills. While teachers typically have excellent skills in the areas of verbal presentation, explanation, and information giving, they generally have less well-developed skills in the areas of listening, counseling, and assertiveness (Seligman, 2000; Turnbull, Turnbull, Erwin, Soodak, & Shogren, 2011). These skill areas are ones that other professionals, such as school psychologists and counselors, have typically had more training on than teachers, which enables them to assist teachers in developing them. This is important as these skills are essential for working effectively with parents and, therefore, are the main focus of this chapter. Another set of skills that is useful for professional working in schools are those for organizing and leading groups and workshops for parents. Discussion of workshops for parents and of group leadership skills is included at the end of the chapter.

The most important of the skills required for working effectively with parents are the ones needed for effective listening. These include the skills of attentiveness, passive listening, paraphrasing, and active listening. Other interpersonal skills that are needed for communicating with parents and for collaborating with colleagues are assertion skills. These include techniques for making and refusing requests, giving constructive feedback, handling criticism, and problem solving. Also useful are basic counseling skills, particularly if set within a problem-solving model of counseling, which involves listening and assertion skills. To use such a model, teachers must first of all *listen* to what parents have to say, to help them clarify their concerns or ideas. Parents should then be helped to gain a clear *understanding* of the problem situation that they face or goal that they have. Finally, teachers should help parents decide what, if anything, they want to do about their concern or issue, that is, what *action* they wish to take. Possessing the skills required to implement this simple model of counseling will contribute enormously to the ability of teachers to establish a productive working relationship with parents. A three-phase problem-solving counseling model is presented later in this chapter, following the discussion of listening and assertion skills.

G. Hornby, *Parental Involvement in Childhood Education: Building Effective School-Family Partnerships*, DOI 10.1007/978-1-4419-8379-4_7,
© Springer Science+Business Media, LLC 2011

Listening Skills

The skills required for effective listening, namely, attentiveness, passive listening, paraphrasing, and active listening are outlined below and discussed in more detail elsewhere (see Hornby, Hall, & Hall, 2003).

Attentiveness

Effective listening requires a high level of attentiveness. This involves focusing one's physical attention on the person being listened to and includes several components, which are outlined below.

Eye Contact

The importance for the listener of maintaining good eye contact cannot be overemphasized. While parents are talking they may not look directly at the listener for most of the time but will occasionally look across to check that he or she is listening. Therefore, it is important to maintain eye contact throughout the interview. In situations where someone feels uncomfortable with direct eye contact, it is usually satisfactory for the listener to look at the speakers' mouth or the tip of their nose instead. Speakers generally cannot tell the difference.

Facing Squarely

To communicate attentiveness, it is important for the listener to face the other person squarely or at a slight angle. Turning one's body away from another person suggests that you are not totally paying attention to them.

Leaning Forward

Leaning slightly forward toward the person being listened to communicates attentiveness. Alternatively, leaning backward gives the impression that you are not listening, so it should be avoided.

Open Posture

Having one's legs crossed, or even worse one's arms crossed, when one is listening gives the impression of a lack of openness, as if a barrier is being placed between the listener and the person talking. Attentiveness is best communicated by the adoption of an open posture with both arms and legs uncrossed.

Remaining Relaxed

It is essential to be relaxed while adopting an attentive posture, since if the posture adopted is not comfortable it is not possible to concentrate fully on what is being said. Therefore, it is important to take up an attentive posture in which one feels relaxed, even if this does not exactly follow the guidelines discussed above.

Appropriate Body Motion

It is important to avoid distracting movements such as looking at the clock, fiddling with a pen, or constantly changing position. In addition, it is important to move appropriately in response to the speaker since a listener who sits perfectly still can be quite unnerving and may not communicate attentiveness.

Nondistracting Environment

It is not easy to listen attentively in an environment in which there are distractions. The room used should be as quiet as possible, and the door should be kept closed. Telephone calls should be put on hold and a "meeting in progress" sign hung on the door. Within the room, the chairs used should be comfortable and there should be no physical barriers, such as desks or tables, between parents and the professional who is listening.

Distance

There needs to be a suitable distance between the speaker and the listener. If the distance is too great or too small, then the speaker will feel uncomfortable and this will impede the communication. A distance of about 3 ft is usually recommended, but this can vary between cultures, so it is best to always look for signs of discomfort or anxiety in the listener and adjust the distance accordingly.

Passive Listening

Passive listening involves using a high level of attentiveness combined with other skills. These are invitations to talk, nonverbal grunts, open questions, attentive silence, avoiding communication blocks, and minimizing self-listening.

Invitations to Talk

Before the professional can begin to listen, parents need to be invited to talk about their concern or issue. For example, "How can I help you?" or "You seem upset. Would you like to talk about it?" The specific wording of the invitation needs to be tailored to the situation and people involved.

Nonverbal Grunts

There are various sounds or short words that are often known as "nonverbal grunts" because they let the speaker know that you are paying attention to them without interrupting the flow. For example, "Go on," "Right," "Huh Huh," "Mm Mm." It is particularly important to use these while listening to someone on the telephone because the speaker cannot gauge the listener's attentiveness through the usual visual clues.

Open Questions

Open questions are used for clarification or to encourage the speaker to continue: For example, "How do you mean?" or "What happened then?" Closed questions, which usually require a very brief response such as "yes" or "no" and allow the listener to set the agenda, should be avoided. This can be very hard for teachers to do since they typically spend much of their time in classrooms asking closed questions and it is difficult to change this strategy quickly.

Attentive Silence

Listeners should pause for a few seconds after each thing they say to give parents the opportunity to say more or to remain silent. During silences, parents are often clarifying their thoughts and feelings. Therefore, using attentive silence is a very effective way of encouraging people to open up and continue exploring their concerns or issues.

Avoiding Communication Blocks

Certain types of comment tend to act as blocks to the communication process and, therefore, should be avoided (Gordon, 1970). When used, they stop parents from exploring their concerns and ideas. A common example is *reassurance*, such as saying, "Don't worry, it will work out all right." Other types of blocks that are particularly annoying to parents are *denial* or *false acknowledgment of feelings,* such as suggesting that parents should "Look on the bright side" or telling them,

"I know exactly how you feel." More blatant blocks to communication are *criticism, sarcasm,* and *advice giving.* Other common blocks involve *diverting* parents from the topic, either directly or by the use of *excessive questioning* or by *excessive self-disclosure* when people go on about themselves or others they have known who have had similar problems. Further blocks involve *moralizing, ordering,* or *threatening,* that is, telling parents what they ought or must do. Finally, there are the blocks in which *diagnosis* or *labeling* are used. For example, telling someone that he or she is "*a worrier.*" All the blocks tend to stifle the exploration of concerns or ideas and therefore should be avoided.

Avoiding Self-Listening

Self-listening occurs when people drift off into their own thoughts rather than listening to what the other person is saying. When a professional is listening to a parent and begins to self-listen, there is a likelihood that important aspects of what is said will be missed. The listener may then become confused and will be unable to respond effectively to the parent, who will therefore become aware of the inadequacy of the listening and tend to clam up. This is why it is very important that when professionals are listening to parents they should be able to reduce self-listening to a minimum. The best way of minimizing self-listening is to use the listening techniques discussed below.

Paraphrasing

Paraphrasing is a skill that most people already use to some extent. When someone has told us something important and we want to be sure that we have understood correctly, we feed back the main points of the message to the person for confirmation. This is a crude form of paraphrasing, which is similar to that used by competent listeners.

An effective paraphrase has four components. *First,* the paraphrase feeds back only the key points of the speaker's message. *Second,* paraphrasing is concerned with the factual content of the speaker's message, not with feelings. *Third,* an effective paraphrase is short and to the point. It is a summary of the speaker's key message, not a summary of everything said. *Fourth,* a paraphrase is stated in the listener's own words, but in a language that is familiar to the speaker.

Paraphrases are used when there are natural breaks in the interaction, such as when the speaker pauses and looks at the listener or when the speaker inflects his or her voice at the end of a sentence, clearly wanting some response from the listener. At this point, the listener feeds back the essence of the speaker's message and then waits for a response. When the paraphrase hits the mark, the speaker typically indicates that this is the case by saying, "That's it" or "Right" or "Yes" or by some nonverbal means such as nodding his or her head. If the paraphrase is not accurate, or only partly accurate, then the response will not be so positive and in most cases the speaker will correct the listener. In doing so, the speaker will also be clarifying for himself or herself exactly what is meant, so the paraphrase will still be of value.

Active listening

Active listening involves trying to understand what the person is feeling and what the key message is in what they are saying, then putting this understanding in your own words and feeding it back to the person (Gordon, 1970). Thus, active listening involves the listener being actively engaged in clarifying the thoughts and feelings of the person they are listening to. It builds on attentiveness, passive listening, and also paraphrasing, in that the main aspects of what is being communicated are reflected back to the person. This is done to provide a kind of "sounding board" to facilitate exploration and clarification of the person's concerns, ideas, and feelings.

Gordon (1970) suggested that certain attitudes are essential prerequisites to active listening. These are as follows:

- The listener must really want to hear what the other person has to say.
- The listener must sincerely want to help the other person with his or her concern.
- The listener must be able to respect the other person's feelings, opinions, attitudes or values even though they may conflict with his or her own.
- The listener must have faith in the other person's ability to work through and solve his or her own problems.
- The listener must realize that feelings are transitory and not be afraid when people express strong feelings such as anger or sadness.

The process of active listening involves reflecting both thoughts and feelings back to the speaker. The speaker's key feeling is fed back along with the apparent reason for the feeling. When learning how to use active listening, it is useful to have a set formula to follow. The formula *"You feel....because....."* is typically used.

For example

"You *feel* frustrated *because* you haven't finished the job,"
"You *feel* delighted *because* she has done so well."

When people gain confidence in their use of active listening, the formula is no longer needed, and thoughts and feelings can be reflected back in a more natural way, for example: "You *are* angry *about* the way you were treated," *"You're* sad *that* it has come to an end," "You *were* pleased *with* the result," and "You *were* annoyed *by* her manner."

However, active listening involves much more than simply using this formula. It requires the listener to set aside his or her own perspective to understand what the other person is experiencing. It therefore involves being aware of how things are said, the expressions and gestures used, and, most importantly, hearing what is not said but that lies behind what is said. The real art in active listening is in feeding this awareness back to the person accurately and sensitively. This, of course, is very difficult, but the beauty of active listening is that you do not have to be completely right to be helpful. An active listening response that is a little off the mark typically gets speakers to clarify their thoughts and feelings further. However, active listening responses that are way off the mark suggest to the speaker that the other person is not listening and therefore can act as blocks to communication.

Assertion Skills

Assertiveness involves being able to stand up for one's own rights while respecting the rights of others and being able to communicate one's ideas, concerns, and needs directly, persistently and diplomatically. It also involves being able to express both positive and negative feelings with openness and honesty, as well as being able to choose how to react to situations from a range of options.

Teachers and other professionals, such as psychologists and counselors, need assertion skills both for working with parents and for collaborating with their colleagues. Teachers will have to deal with criticism or aggression from time to time and will need to make and refuse requests. They will also need to be able to give constructive feedback. Finally, they will need to be able to help solve problems. The skills involved in these situations are outlined below and are discussed in more detail elsewhere (Hornby, 1994).

Basic Elements of Assertiveness

There are three aspects of assertiveness that apply in any situation. These are physical assertiveness, vocal assertiveness, and assertion muscle levels.

Physical Assertiveness

Assertive body language is a key component of effective assertion. The components of physical assertiveness are similar to those of the attentiveness required for effective listening: an open posture, facing the other person squarely, standing or sitting erect or leaning slightly forward, maintaining good eye contact, not fidgeting or using superfluous gestures. What is different about assertiveness is that the facial expression should match the seriousness of the message and also that feet should be firmly planted on the floor, even when sitting.

Vocal Assertiveness

To optimize the effectiveness of the message, one's voice should be firm but calm. It is best to speak a little more slowly than usual but at a normal volume and to breath deeply as this will help to ensure that there is enough breath to speak firmly and to maintain calmness.

Assertion Muscle Levels

Whenever one is being assertive, it is important to select the appropriate strength or "muscle level" of the assertive response used. Usually, one should start at the lowest muscle level, or assertion strength, which is likely to achieve success, for example, "I would appreciate it if you could...." If this does not work, the muscle level is increased and the request repeated, for example, "It is important that you...." Muscle levels are then progressively increased until a satisfactory response is obtained, for example, from "It is essential that you....." to, finally, "I demand that you...."

At the same time when verbal muscle levels are being increased, physical and vocal assertiveness should also be gradually made more intense, that is, by using a more serious facial expression and a firmer tone of voice with each increase in muscle level.

Responding to Criticism

Professionals will occasionally get criticism from their colleagues and sometimes from parents. Important factors involved in determining the impact of criticism are the intention of the person giving it and whether it comes with constructive suggestions for change. Holland and Ward (1990) have described a four-step approach that is useful in considering how to respond to criticism. The four steps of the model are outlined below.

Step One: Listening to the Criticism

Listening skills are useful in clarifying the criticism. Open questions such as "How do you mean?" or "Can you be more specific?" are helpful in finding out exactly what the criticism is aimed at.

Step Two: Deciding on the Truth

Before responding to the criticism, its validity should be considered. It may be completely true, partly true, or completely untrue. One's assessment of the validity of the criticism will determine the response used in step three.

Step Three: Responding Assertively

If we consider the criticism to be completely true, then it is best to agree with the criticizer, make a brief apology, and assure them you will correct the situation, for example, "I'm sorry about not consulting you on this matter. I'll make sure it doesn't happen again."

If we consider the criticism is partly true, then we should agree with the part considered to be valid, briefly apologize, and at the same time correct the part that is false, for example, "Yes, I did make a mistake in that case and I regret that, but I don't accept that I'm making mistakes all the time these days. I make occasional errors like anyone else."

If we consider the criticism to be completely false then we should clearly reject it, tell the other person exactly how the criticism makes us feel, ask for an explanation of their comments, and make an affirmative statement about ourselves, for example, "I don't agree that I was wrong in that case and am greatly offended by the suggestion. What grounds could you possibly have for making such a comment? My relationships with pupils are excellent."

Step Four: Letting Go

Decide to use what you have learned from the criticism and about the criticizer and move on. This is "much easier said than done," but we mustn't let ourselves be deflected from our goals by what is, after all, just one person's opinion.

Dealing with Aggression

Occasionally, professionals, especially teachers, have to deal with aggressive behavior from parents or colleagues. Kroth (1985) has provided some guidelines for what teachers should do and should not do in this situation.

Teachers Should Not:

- Argue with a person who is behaving aggressively
- Raise their voices or begin to shout
- Become defensive and feel they have to defend their position
- Attempt to minimize the concern that the other person is expressing
- Take responsibility for problems that are not of their making
- Make promises that they will not be able to fulfill

All of these responses are ones that are commonly used by people confronted with aggression, but they seldom work and are more likely to inflame the situation and make the other person more aggressive. The following responses are far more likely to calm the other person down and lead to a constructive resolution of the situation.

Teachers Should:

- Actively listen to the other person, reflecting back their thoughts and feelings to confirm that you are listening and to help you understand their perspective
- Speak softly, slowly, and calmly
- Ask for clarification of any complaints that are vague
- Ask what else is bothering them in order to exhaust their list of complaints
- Make a list of their concerns. Read out the list and ask if it is correct and complete

- Use the techniques of problem solving, discussed below, to work through the list of concerns in order to resolve the problems or conflicts, starting with the one of highest priority to the other person

Refusing a Request

Professionals will sometimes receive requests from parents or colleagues that they think they should not agree to but feel unable to turn down. People have difficulty saying *"no"* for several reasons but especially due to the fear that it will damage their relationship with the other person. The alternative to agreeing to requests you would rather turn down is to use acceptable ways of saying *"no,"* several of which are listed below.

The Explained "No"

When you have a genuine reason for the refusal, you can say "no," explain why you are turning down the request, and give a brief apology, for example, "No, I'm sorry, I can't make it because I'm already booked for that day."

The Postponed "No"

In this refusal, you explain that you cannot comply with the request at present but may be able to in the future, for example, "No, I'm sorry, I'm not able to take that on today, but I may be able to help you with it in the future."

The Delayed "No"

In this technique, you ask for time to think it over. This gives you the opportunity to carefully consider whether you want to comply with the request and to work out exactly how you will say "no," for example, "I'm busy right now and I'd like to give it some thought. Can I get back to you tomorrow?"

The Listening "No"

In this refusal, active listening skills are used to let other people know that you understand the reason for their request. The listening response is combined with a brief apology and a firm refusal, for example, "Yes I understand your frustration about not being able to get the job done. I'm sorry, but I can't help you with it."

The "Get Back to Me" "No"

This involves explaining the difficulties you have in complying with the request. Then suggesting that the person try elsewhere and if all else fails to get back to you and you will see what you can do, for example, "I'm busy for the next 2 weeks so I suggest you try elsewhere. If you really get stuck I'll do my best to fit you in but I can't promise anything."

The "Broken Record" "No"

This form of refusal is particularly useful for dealing with people who will not take "no" for an answer. It involves making a brief statement of refusal to the other person, avoiding getting into discussion with them, and simply repeating the statement as many times as necessary (like a broken record) until the message gets across. Typically, it takes only one or two repetitions to get the message across.

Making a Request

Professionals sometimes need to request various things from their colleagues and occasionally need to make requests of parents. So, being able to make requests effectively is important, especially, since many people find it difficult to do. Manthei (1981) has provided some useful guidelines for making requests and these are outlined below.

- *State your request directly* – state your request firmly and clearly to the other person.
- *Say exactly what you want* – be specific and precise about your requirements.
- *Focus on the positive* – create an expectation of compliance.
- *Answer only questions seeking clarification* – do not allow yourself to be sidetracked.
- *Allow the person time to think about it* – suggest you will get back to them tomorrow.
- *Repeat the request* – use the "broken record" technique to restate the request.
- *Be prepared to compromise* – You are better off getting partial agreement than rejection.
- *Realize the other person has the right to refuse* – respect the other person's rights.

Giving Constructive Feedback

Giving constructive feedback to others is an important skill for both our professional and personal lives. Whereas criticism is mostly given without the intention of helping the other person, constructive feedback is aimed at helping them to function better.

A model for providing constructive feedback that is extremely useful is one adapted from the DESC script popularized by Bower and Bower (1976). DESC stands for describe, express (or explain), specify, and consequences. This is a technique that many professionals find valuable in giving feedback to parents as well as their colleagues. Parents also find it useful in handling difficulties with professionals. The four steps involved in using the modified DESC script are described below.

Describe

Describe the behavior of concern in the most specific and objective terms possible, for example, "When you change teaching programs without consulting me...."

Express or Explain

Either express your feelings about this behavior or explain the difficulties it causes for you, or do both, calmly and positively, without blaming or judging the other person, or "putting them down," for example, "....I get very annoyed (express) because parents may become confused and even lose confidence in us" (explain).

Specify

Specify the exact change in behavior required of the other person, for example, "...So, in future, will you make sure you consult me before making such changes...".

Consequences

The consequences that are likely to result from the other person complying with the request are stated. The benefits for both people involved are stated first, then benefits for others, for example, "...Then, we will be able to maintain our excellent working relationship and parents will be clear about our teaching programs."

If the other person is not willing to comply, then the modified DESC script should be repeated at progressively higher muscle levels including the negative consequences for the person of not complying with the request, for example, "...If you do not consult me as I suggest then I will have to insist on all your teaching plans being formally submitted to me for approval."

Preparation and Delivery

Although the modified DESC script is simple enough to be thought up and delivered on the spot, it is usually best to write it out beforehand. It is then possible to make sure that the wording is the most appropriate and also to rehearse it with a third person to get a feedback on it. It can then be decided when, where, and how it can best be delivered.

Problem Solving

Often professionals find that their opinions differ from those of parents or their colleagues. This can lead to deterioration in relationships, unless these difficulties are resolved. Bolton (1979) has proposed a model for solving problems that is useful in this situation. The six steps of the model are described below.

Define Problem in Terms of Needs of Each Person

This involves the use of active listening to clarify the other person's needs and, if possible, to understand the reason for these needs. It also involves stating one's own needs assertively. This is a key element of the model and may take up half of the total time required for the process.

Brainstorming Possible Solutions

Once both persons' needs are understood brainstorming can be used to seek solutions that meet both sets of needs. First, as many potential solutions as possible should be listed, without attempting to evaluate or clarify any of them. Wild ideas should be included as these often help generate more creative solutions. Then, each other's ideas should be expanded on and clarified.

Select Solutions That Meet Both Party's Needs

A choice is then made from the list of potential solutions, of the one that best meets the needs of both parties. This will probably involve discussing the relative merits of several solutions in meeting each other's needs.

Plan Who Will Do What, Where, and When

It is useful to make a written note of the decision about what each party will do, where it will be done and when it will be completed by.

Implement the Plan

It is clearly important that each party should attempt to follow the agreement precisely in implementing the plan.

Evaluate the Process and the Solution

An essential part of the problem-solving process is to agree a time when both parties can meet to evaluate how well the solution is meeting each of their needs.

Counseling Skills

The counseling model that is proposed for use with parents is based on a general approach to counseling that can be used with children and adults in a wide variety of situations. The model involves a three phase approach to counseling with phases of *listening, understanding*, and *action planning*. It is a problem-solving approach to counseling adapted from previous models by Egan (1982) and Allan and Nairne (1984) and is presented in more detail elsewhere (Hornby, 1994).

The majority of parents will not ask for counseling directly, but will typically go to teachers with concerns about their children. If teachers use listening skills to help parents explore their concerns, then the parents' need for help will emerge. This is when teachers should be able to help parents by providing the counseling that they need. Parents are much more likely to be willing to talk about their concerns with someone who is working directly with their child, such as a teacher, than with a professional counselor who they do not know. What teachers need therefore is a counseling model that is practical, simple to learn, and easy to use. They also need to have contact with professionals, such as psychologists or counselors, who can support them in its use and be someone teachers can refer on to when situations start to go beyond their level of competence. A summary of the model proposed is presented in Fig. 7.1.

The rationale for using such a model is based on the idea that any problem or concern that parents raise with teachers can be dealt with by taking them through the three phases of the model in order to help them find the solution that best suits their needs. First of all, the teacher uses the skills of the *listening* phase to establish

STAGE	LISTENING	UNDERSTANDING	ACTION PLANNING
SKILLS	Attentiveness	Structuring	Brainstorming options
		Summarising	Evaluating options
	Passive Listening	Identifying Themes	Action planning skills
		Expressing Implications	
	Paraphrasing	Information giving	Assertion skills
		Suggesting alternative interpretations	
		Suggesting new perspectives	Reviewing skills
	Active Listening	Goal setting	Termination skills

Direction of Movement in Counseling Process

Fig. 7.1 Three phase counseling model

a working relationship with parents, to help them open up and to explore any concerns they have. Then, the teacher moves on to the second phase, using the skills of the *understanding* phase to help parents get a clearer picture of their concerns, develop new perspectives on their situation, and suggest possible goals for change. Finally, the teacher moves on to the third phase, of *action planning,* in which possible options for solving parents' problems are examined and plans for action are developed. Thus, different skills are needed at each phase of the model: Skills for listening in the first phase, skills for understanding in the second phase and skills for action planning in the third phase. These are discussed below.

Skills for Listening

The first phase of the model involves the use of the listening skills that are described earlier in this chapter. *Attentiveness* and *passive listening* are used to establish a rapport to help parents open up. *Paraphrasing* and *active listening* are used to help parents explore their concerns and issues.

Skills for Understanding

The second phase of the model involves the use of skills designed to increase the parent's understanding of their problem situation. Skills used to help parents get a clearer picture of their concerns include: *structuring,* which involves keeping parents focused on key aspects of their concern; *summarizing,* which involves feeding back to parents an overview of their key thoughts and feelings; *identifying themes,* which involves feeding back to parents any common themes, connections or contradictions running through their account of the situation they are concerned about; *expressing implications*, which involves drawing tentative conclusions about the parent's situation and linking this with the possible implications of these conclusions; and *information giving,* which involves teachers sharing with parents, either from their experience of children or from other knowledge relevant to the parent's situation.

Skills used to help parents develop new perspectives on their situation include the following: *suggesting alternative interpretations,* which involves suggesting objective explanations for past events to counter the negative interpretations which parents are sometimes held back by, and *suggesting new perspectives*, which involves helping parents to consider more constructive ways of viewing their situation.

Finally, to help parents develop possible goals for change, the skill of *goal setting* is used. This involves helping parents decide on the major aspect of their situation that needs to be focused on and considering potential changes that are desirable and feasible.

Skills for Action Planning

The third phase of the model involves the use of action planning skills to help parents consider possible options for addressing their concerns, develop plans for action, and review the progress of these plans. The skills used to help parents consider possible options for change are the same ones used in the problem-solving model discussed earlier in this chapter. They include the skills of *brainstorming options* and *evaluating options*.

Once parents have decided on their preferred option, *action planning skills* are used to help them develop concrete plans for implementing this option. In addition, parents can be taught some of the *assertion skills*, discussed earlier in this chapter, to help them implement this plan.

Next, *reviewing skills* are used to help parents to review the progress of these plans. This involves arranging for further contact to evaluate parents' progress with their plans. If there has been insufficient progress, then the process can be recycled and parents are once more taken through the three phases of the model to develop a new action plan.

Finally, *termination skills* are used to refer parents on for more specialist help, or to bring to a close a successful series of contacts, while communicating to parents that they are welcome to return to discuss other concerns at any stage in the future.

Group Leadership Skills

One of the less well-developed aspects of parental involvement in the schools surveyed was parent education. Some of the schools did report organizing parent education workshops, but there were not very many of these. It is considered that this is probably because teachers have not had training in the skills needed to lead workshops with parents. Therefore, it is important for professionals such as psychologists, social workers, and counselors who work in schools to collaborate with teachers in providing such workshops, thereby assisting teachers to develop the necessary group leadership skills. The benefits of group work with parents are discussed below, followed by an outline of the knowledge and skills needed to lead workshops for parents, which are discussed in more detail elsewhere (see Hornby, 1994).

Benefits of Group Work with Parents

The most important benefit of working with groups of parents is that, in talking with others, parents realize that they are not the only ones with concerns about their children. In addition, parents can express their feelings regarding their children and discover that others have similar feelings, which often helps them come to terms with their own.

Further, in a group with other parents it is often easier for them to reveal concerns that they have not felt able to bring up individually. Another benefit of group work is that parents experience mutual support from the other group members, which helps them to become more confident in their own ability as parents. A further benefit of group work is that when parents participate in a group they learn together in a mutually supportive atmosphere and are often more responsive to changing their opinions and learning new strategies in this situation.

There are also advantages of working with groups of parents for the teachers involved. Obviously, since more parents can be reached in a group than individually, it is possible to help a greater number of parents than could be managed through individual parent–teacher meetings. Also, there are times when several parents are experiencing the same difficulty and teachers can provide guidance to them all at the same time rather than individually, thereby using their time more efficiently. Another advantage is that, because of the efficient use of time in group work, it is possible to justify two or more professionals working together with the group of parents and thereby sharing skills and knowledge with each other. In addition, coleading parent workshops with psychologists or counselors is a powerful way for teachers to learn new skills and gain a greater understanding of parents' experiences and needs.

However, there are some negative aspects of doing group work with parents. Some parents do not feel comfortable being in a group with other parents and prefer to receive counseling or guidance individually. Also, in order to obtain maximum participation in group work with parents it is often necessary to hold sessions in evenings or at the weekend, which can cut into teachers' leisure and preparation time. Finally, working with groups of parents requires skills and knowledge over and above that needed for individual work, so these need to be acquired to a reasonable level before embarking on group work with parents (Seligman, 2000). Group leadership skills and knowledge of group dynamics are discussed next.

Group Leadership Skills

The main skills needed to lead workshops for parents include those discussed above, that is, counseling skills, assertion skills, and, most importantly, listening skills. However, the skills required to lead such groups are more comprehensive than those needed for individual work with parents. Dinkmeyer and Muro (1979) suggest that, first and foremost, group leaders need to be skilled listeners. They suggest that leaders also need to be able to develop trust within the group and to maintain a focus on the goals of both the group as a whole and of the individuals within it. Further, leaders need to be spontaneous and to be responsive to what is happening within the group at any point in time. They need to be able to combine the ability to stand firm with a good sense of humor. Finally, to be effective, they need to be perceived by group members as being with them as a group and for them as individuals.

A useful perspective on leadership skills is that provided by Trotzer (1977) who considers that group leaders need the skills of *reaction, interaction,* and *action.* These are briefly outlined below.

The *reaction skills* that leaders need are as follows:

- *Listening*: in order to communicate respect, acceptance, empathy, and caring
- *Restating*: to convey to group members that they are being heard
- *Reflecting*: in order to convey understanding and help members to express themselves
- *Clarifying*: in order to better understand confusing aspects of what is said
- *Summarizing*: to provide an overview, stimulate reactions, and move on to new ground

The *interaction skills* that leaders need are as follows:

- *Moderating*: to ensure that all group members have the opportunity to talk
- *Interpreting*: to help members gain insight into what is happening within the group
- *Linking*: to tie together common elements within the group and promote cohesiveness
- *Blocking*: to prevent undesirable action by one or more group members
- *Supporting*: to encourage members to share of themselves safely within the group
- *Limiting*: to prevent actions which would infringe the rights of group members
- *Protecting*: to prevent group members from being unduly criticized or hurt
- *Consensus taking*: to help members see where they stand in relation to others

The *action skills* that leaders need are as follows:

- *Questioning*: to help group members consider aspects they had not thought of
- *Probing*: to help members look more deeply into their concerns
- *Tone setting*: to establish a healthy atmosphere within the group
- *Confronting*: to help members face things about themselves which they are avoiding
- *Personal sharing*: to show that the leader is human and is prepared to open up
- *Modeling*: to teach members interpersonal skills such as active listening

Group Dynamics

In addition to these skills, leaders of parent workshops also need to have a good understanding of group dynamics, that is, the processes that occur within groups. Models of group dynamics or the process of group development suggest that all groups need to pass through several stages or phases if they are to function well and achieve their goals. Williamson (1982) suggests that there are four phases of group development: *inclusion, work, action,* and *termination.* These are outlined below.

Inclusion

The first phase of any group is one of developing group cohesiveness so that all members feel a part of the group. Participants need to feel comfortable about belonging to the group. They need to be willing to share aspects of themselves and to explore concerns and issues within the group. Some time will be needed for this to develop as members initially interact tentatively with group leaders and each other. As this process develops, group norms or implicit group rules will begin to be established.

Work

The second phase is one in which the members begin to work on resolving the concerns or issues related to the purpose of the group. This is usually the longest phase in the group's life. It involves members in discussing ideas, expressing feelings, and listening to others to gain insight into their own situation. It is in this phase that group members will experience the greatest benefit. However, some members will resist change, and there will be conflict and tension within the group. At the same time, relationships between other group members will deepen and become more meaningful. The work phase can be regarded as providing a transition between members becoming part of the group and deciding what action to take.

Action

In the third phase, the understanding and growth that occurs in the work phase needs to be translated into some form of action; otherwise, the group will not fulfill its purpose. Individual members, or the group as a whole, need to decide what action to take to address the concerns that brought them into the group. Since change is difficult for members to cope with, the group needs to provide them with considerable support during this phase.

Termination

The final phase is one in which the group comes to a close with members experiencing a sense of completion, accomplishment and gratitude for what the group has helped them achieve.

When groups progress through these four phases then the experience can be a very powerful one in promoting learning and personal growth in the members. I have observed this happen on numerous occasions with parents who have participated in parent workshops. The growth in confidence of many parents over the period of these projects has often been startling. Unfortunately, however, since groups can be so powerful, when they are badly led, they can result in members having their self-confidence threatened. So, it is essential to ensure that qualified and experienced leaders are employed for any group work carried out with parents. This is why it is useful for teachers to team up with school psychologists or counselors to colead parent workshops.

Organization of Parent Groups and Workshops

A summary of the main aspects of workshop organization is presented below.

Recruitment

The best method of recruiting parents for workshops is by sending a letter of invitation to all parents likely to be concerned with the topic being addressed, whose children are attending the school.

Venue

A venue that is familiar to the parents, comfortable, and easy for parents to get to is best. School staff rooms are a popular choice of venue for smaller workshops, and school halls for larger ones.

Sessions

Workshops with parents can be organized as half-day or whole-day events. However, a series of shorter sessions is generally more effective as it benefits from the process of group development described above. Between six and eight, weekly, two hour, evening sessions are generally the most satisfactory. Less than six sessions is too few for parents to benefit from the therapeutic process that the group will experience as the workshop progresses. More than eight sessions is often too great a commitment of time for parents. Anything greater than a 1-week break between sessions, such as fortnightly or monthly sessions, can lead to a considerable drop in attendance and therefore should be avoided. Evening sessions are generally easier for both professionals and parents to attend, but weekends can also be used. Two hours is considered to be the optimum time for the length of sessions. Any less leaves insufficient time for both discussion and presentation of information by professionals.

Number of Parents

A large number of parents can be catered for by taking the group of parents as a whole during the introduction, presentations, and final summary sections of the workshop and dividing them into small groups during the discussion section. The size of the small groups needs to be large enough to give a reasonable diversity of parents but small enough to provide sufficient time for each parent to discuss his or her concern. About six to ten parents in a group is generally the most satisfactory size.

Group Leaders

Group discussions need to be led by professionals with previous experience of leading such groups such as psychologists or counselors. Teachers with no experience can be involved as coleaders who work in tandem with the leader. In this way, teachers can be trained to lead their own groups in subsequent parent workshops.

Format for Parent Workshops

The type of parent workshops that I have found most effective is one that consists of four sections: introduction, lecture presentation, small group discussion, and summary. These are outlined below.

Introduction

The first 15 min of workshops are used to help parents relax, since many of them experience anxiety when they first come along to group sessions where they are expected to talk about their children. It provides an opportunity for parents to get to know other parents as well as teachers and other professionals involved informally and also overcomes the problem of late arrivals interrupting the lecture presentations.

Lecture Presentations

Lecture-type presentations of a maximum of 20 min in length are presented to the whole group of parents who are usually seated in a horseshoe arrangement around the speaker. The topics of the lectures are best determined by surveying parents beforehand. Where necessary, relevant specialists can then be invited in to give some of the lectures.

Small Group Discussions

The largest block of time in workshops, of over an hour, is given over to discussion that is conducted in small groups. Discussions are conducted in separate rooms, with chairs arranged in a circle. Groups usually consist of a leader, a coleader, and six to ten parents. Leaders guide the discussions using the skills discussed above. Coleaders work in tandem with leaders by focusing on the group dynamics and on the body language of group members so that they can draw the leader's attention to a parent who may want to say something but has not been noticed.

Summary

With all the parents present, a leader or coleader from each small group reports back on the issues and concerns discussed in their group. Any handouts, such as a summary of the lecture content for that session, are distributed and homework tasks, are explained. It is important to conclude the formal aspects of each session punctually, since many parents will have arranged babysitters and need to be home promptly. However, it has been found that some parents will remain to talk with other parents or professionals for up to half an hour afterward. Leaders and coleaders should meet for half an hour before each session to plan the session and for a short time afterwards to debrief and plan subsequent sessions.

Summary and Conclusion

Professionals such as educational psychologists, school counselors, and teachers need to have good interpersonal communication skills to work effectively with parents. Listening, assertion and counseling skills have, therefore, been elaborated in this chapter. The skills required for effective listening that are discussed include attentiveness, passive listening, paraphrasing, and active listening. The assertion skills that are described include techniques for making and refusing requests, giving constructive feedback, handling criticism, and problem solving. The basic counseling skills that are discussed were set within a three-phase problem-solving model of counseling that involves listening, understanding, and action planning skills. The knowledge and skills required for working with groups of parents are outlined, including the benefits of group work, leadership skills, group dynamics, and the format and organization of parent workshops.

Chapter 8
Role of Professionals in Improving Parental Involvement

Introduction

This book focuses on the importance of parental involvement in the education of their children and on the key role that professionals, especially school and educational psychologists, can play in supporting teachers and schools to develop effective involvement strategies and activities for parents. Other professionals, including school counselors and social workers, can also make important contributions, but it is argued that school and educational psychologists are the ones whose training and roles in the education system make them ideally placed to provide guidance to schools, teachers, and parents on developing effective involvement.

As Karther and Lowden (1997) have suggested, "Although the rewards are great, parent involvement presents numerous challenges to educators (p. 41)." One of the challenges is to overcome, or reduce, the impact of the various barriers to parental involvement that were discussed in Chap. 2. Another is to develop a partnership approach and adopt a model to guide the implementation of this partnership, as discussed in Chap. 3. A key challenge is to address the potential gaps in schools' provision of parental involvement that were identified in the findings of the research studies reported in Chaps. 4 and 5. Further challenges are to provide training and support to enable teachers to develop competence in the parental involvement strategies described in Chap. 6 as well as the various skills required for implementing the strategies discussed in Chap. 7.

However, from an ecological perspective, psychologists will only be able to provide guidance and support for teachers to improve parental involvement organized by schools if the environment in which they work values parental involvement in education. Various components at different levels of overall education systems all have a part to play in determining how effectively parents are involved in the education of their children. Attention must therefore be paid to the role of psychologists with respect to all components in the process of improving parent involvement. These components operate at four levels of the overall education systems in each

G. Hornby, *Parental Involvement in Childhood Education: Building Effective School-Family Partnerships*, DOI 10.1007/978-1-4419-8379-4_8,
© Springer Science+Business Media, LLC 2011

country: government, local education system, school, and teacher. Psychologists have important roles to play in developments at each of these levels to bring about long-term improvements in parental involvement.

Ecological Perspective on Improving Parental Involvement

Government

Legislation

The necessity for parental involvement in education must be mandated by appropriate legislation, which is now the case in countries such as England and USA. Countries in which this is not the case need to make it a priority, since it not possible to achieve high levels of parental involvement, unless this is required by the laws of the land. Professionals, including school psychologists, who work with parents, have a key role to play in advocating for such legislation. They should also support parents in advocating for appropriate legislation, as the lobbying carried out by parent groups and organizations often has greater impact on politicians responsible for enacting legislation than lobbying by professionals.

Policy and Research

There needs to be a national policy on parental involvement in education that clearly sets out expectations for education systems, schools, teachers, and parents. Psychologists can contribute to policy formation by making sure that they keep policy makers up to date with the research literature on parental involvement so that policy can be based on evidence of effective practice. Psychologists should also contribute to the research literature by conducting studies on aspects of parental involvement of particular relevance to the communities in which they work, such as the views of teachers and parents on the parental involvement organized by schools, or the role of schools in educating parents about the importance of home-based parental involvement.

Resources

Governments need to provide sufficient finance to ensure that all components necessary to facilitate high levels of parental involvement can function efficiently. This includes money for both human and physical resources. Although teachers are at the forefront of parental involvement activities, professionals such as school and educational psychologists, social workers and school counselors are important resources for supporting teachers and schools in implementing effective involvement strategies and activities.

Public Awareness

Governments need to disseminate the details of existing legislation, policies, and resources available to education systems, schools, teachers, and parents. This can be done through advertisements in the media, circulars to schools and education authorities as well as leaflets for parents distributed through schools, libraries, and health centers. As part of their broader roles in education systems, psychologists can assist in the dissemination process by making sure that the school staff and parents they interact with have all the relevant information they need.

Education System

Policy

Education systems need to have a clear policy for parent involvement that draws on national policy and adapts this to local conditions and needs. Education administrators should involve psychologists in the development and implementation of effective policies for parental involvement because they are the professionals most likely to have the necessary training and skills to assist with this.

Procedures for Improving Parental Involvement

Education systems must have procedures in place for supporting schools in the implementation of policies for improving parent involvement. They need to have staff that monitor what is happening in schools and offer support and guidance regarding the implementation of good practice with respect to parental involvement. These staff need to understand that second-order change is required to bring about changes in schools' provision for parental involvement (Rosenthal & Sawyers, 1996). This requires a reevaluation of the basis for involving parents and a willingness to try new approaches. It involves an alteration in assumptions about working with parents, as well as the implementation of some different strategies for parent involvement.

Resources

Education systems must commit sufficient resources to ensure the effective implementation of their policy and procedures for parental involvement. For example, many countries, such as the USA and England, now have parent partnership schemes that are designed for this purpose. In addition, some schools have home–school liaison teachers whose function is to improve parental involvement at the school level. In addition, most education systems employ school or educational psychologists who have the skills and knowledge required for optimizing parental involvement in education.

School

Policy

Findings from the surveys of schools reported in Chaps. 4 and 5 indicated that very few schools have written policies for parental involvement. It is considered that each school needs to develop its own policy for parental involvement, encompassing issues from developing a school ethos that promotes working in partnership with parents to providing details of how parents are to contact teachers when they have a concern, as discussed in Chap. 3. Also included must be the methods by which the details of this policy are communicated to parents and the roles of each member of school staff in implementing this policy. School policies for parental involvement should be developed in collaboration with parents of children who attend the school, and with school psychologists.

Procedures

Another key finding from the surveys of schools reported in Chaps. 4 and 5 is the typically ad hoc nature of the organization of parental involvement in the schools. Assisting schools to develop effective organization and procedures for parent involvement is an important role for professionals who work with schools, especially school and educational psychologists whose training equips them for this role. Findings from two studies emphasizes the important leadership role that psychologists can play in helping schools develop effective strategies for parental involvement (Christenson et al., 1997; Pelco et al., 2000). Involving psychologists will help to ensure that the most effective procedures for parental involvement are used by schools to bring about the best possible personal, social, and academic outcomes for children.

Activities

Schools need to use a wide range of activities to achieve the greatest possible involvement of parents. These activities must address parents' needs and contributions at each level of the model for parent involvement presented in Chap. 3 and follow the guidelines for organization of the activities presented in Chap. 6. However, the research reported in Chaps. 4 and 5 found that schools need to focus more on the development of some aspects of working with parents, such as parent education and home visits. Schools also need to make sure that they have procedures in place to ensure the involvement of parents of children with special educational needs. In addition, since another finding reported in Chaps. 4 and 5 was the lack of initiatives for involving parents from diverse backgrounds, it is important for schools to consider activities that will promote this. As suggested by Karther and Lowden (1997, p.41), "… schools may need to reconsider conventional assumptions and practices in order to build bridges to families who do not readily respond to traditional parent–school activities." Psychologists need to support schools in implementing these activities.

Evaluation/Feedback

Schools should continually seek feedback from parents to evaluate the effectiveness of the parent involvement activities that they have in place. Schools should conduct regular needs assessments and surveys on the current involvement of parents, as well as seek suggestions from parents about how their involvement can be made more effective (Rosenthal & Sawyers, 1996). Psychologists can assist schools with the design of these evaluation procedures.

Teacher

Commitment

Teachers need to be committed to working as closely as possible with parents. They need to embody the attitudes of objectivity, sensitivity, genuineness, respect, empathy, and positive yet realistic thinking that are discussed in Chap. 1. This also involves embracing the seven principles of effective partnership discussed in Chap. 3: trust, respect, competence, communication, commitment, equality, and advocacy (Turnbull et al., 2011). Psychologists should demonstrate these attitudes and principles in their interactions with parents and teachers, thereby modeling the commitment required to work effectively with parents.

Knowledge and Skills

Teachers need to understand the impact of the common barriers to parental involvement discussed in Chap. 2 and know about the wide range of strategies for parental involvement discussed in Chap. 6. Teachers also need to develop the skills required for working effectively with parents that were outlined in Chap. 7. Findings from the research reported in Chaps. 4 and 5 indicate that teachers have typically had little training in the knowledge and skills needed to work with parents, either as part of their initial training or as practicing teachers. Therefore, school and educational psychologists have an important role to play in providing training to teachers to enable them to develop this knowledge and skills.

Action

Teachers are the ones who must implement school policy and procedures for parental involvement. Psychologists can provide support to teachers to enable them to develop the confidence to try out different ways of working with parents. Using some of the ideas presented in Chap. 6, events can be organized that will involve the majority of parents of children attending the school. If teachers make a special effort to get to know as many parents as possible at this event, it could be the trigger that leads to improved parent involvement. Parents will then be more open to participating in a whole range of other activities including many of those described in the model for parent involvement proposed in Chap. 3. Teachers need to capitalize on this situation by ensuring that the types of involvement outlined in this model are made available to parents.

Summary and Conclusion

This chapter emphasizes the role that psychologists, and other professionals who work with parents, can play in initiatives to improve parental involvement in schools. It also presented an ecological analysis of the key components involved in improving parental involvement, which focused on changes necessary at the levels of government, education system, school, and teacher. Psychologists have a key role to play in advocating for change at the levels of government and education system, as well as in bringing about changes at the school and teacher levels. It is hoped that the contents of this book will be helpful in these tasks and that psychologists, counselors, social workers, and teachers will feel empowered to take up the challenge of improving parental involvement in education.

References

Adelman, H. (1992). Parents and schools: An intervention perspective. *Eric Digest: ED350645*. Retrieved September 2, 2008 from http://www.eric.ed.gov

Allan, J., & Nairne, J. (1984). *Class discussions for teachers and counsellors in the elementary school*. Toronto: University of Toronto Press.

Atkin, J., Bastiani, J., & Goode, J. (1988). *Listening to parents: An approach to the improvement of home-school relations*. London: Croom Helm.

Baker, J. (1997). Improving parent improvement programs and practice: A qualitative study of teacher perceptions. *School Community Journal, 7*(2), 155–182.

Bastiani, J. (Ed.). (1987). *Parents and teachers 1:Perspectives on home-school relations*. Windsor: NFER-Nelson.

Bastiani, J. (Ed.). (1988). *Parents and teachers 2: From policy to practice*. Windsor: NFER-Nelson.

Bastiani, J. (1989). *Working with parents: A whole school approach*. Windsor: NFER-Nelson.

Bastiani, J. (1993). Parents as partners. Genuine progress or empty rhetoric? In P. Munn (Ed.), *Parents and schools: Customers, managers or partners?* (pp. 101–116). London: Routledge.

Bauch, P. A. (2001). School-community partnerships in rural schools: Leadership, renewal, and a sense of place. *Peabody Journal of Education, 76*, 204–221.

Berger, E. H. (1991). *Parents as partners in education* (3rd ed.). New York: Merrill.

Biddulph, F., Biddulph, J., & Biddulph, C. (2003). *The complexity of community and family influences on children's achievement in New Zealand: Best evidence synthesis*. Wellington: Ministry of Education.

Binns, K., Steinberg, A., & Amorosi, S. (1997). *The Metropolitan Life survey of the American teacher: Building family-school partnerships: Views of teachers and students*. New York: Lewis Harris and Associates.

Blank, M., & Kershaw, C. (Eds.). (1998). *The design book for building partnerships: School, home and community*. Lancaster, PA: Technomic.

Bolton, R. (1979). *People skills*. Englewood Cliffs, NJ: Prentice-Hall.

Boult, B. (2006). *176 ways to involve parents: Practical strategies for partnering with families*. Thousand Oaks, CA: Corwin Press.

Bower, S. A., & Bower, G. H. (1976). *Asserting yourself*. Reading, MA: Addison-Wesley.

Bronfenbrenner, U. (1979). *The ecology of human development*. Cambridge, MA: Harvard University Press.

Bull, A., Brooking, K., & Campbell, R. (2008). *Successful home-school partnerships: Report prepared for the Ministry of Education*. Wellington: MoE.

Catsambis, S. (2001). Expanding knowledge of parental involvement in children's secondary education: Connections with high school seniors' academic success. *Social Psychology of Education, 5*, 149–177.

Chen, J. J. (2008). Grade level differences: Relations of parental, teacher and peer support to academic engagement and achievement among Hong Kong students. *School Psychology International, 29*(2), 183–198.

Christenson, S. L. (2004). The family-school partnership: An opportunity to promote the learning competence of all students. *School Psychology Review, 33*(1), 83–104.

Christenson, S. L., Hurley, C. M., Sheridan, S. M., & Fensternmacher, K. (1997). Parents' and school psychologists' perspectives on parent involvement activities. *School Psychology Review, 26*(1), 111–130.

Christenson, S. L., & Sheridan, S. M. (2001). *Schools and families: Creating essential connections for learning.* New York: Guilford Press.

Clark, R. (1983). *Family life and school achievement: Why poor black children succeed or fail.* Chicago: University of Chicago Press.

Collins, D., Tank, M., & Basith, A. (1993). *Concise guide to customs of minority ethnic religions.* Aldershot: Ashgate.

Cox, D. D. (2005). Evidence-based interventions using home-school collaboration. *School Psychology Quarterly, 20*(4), 473–497.

Cunningham, C., & Davis, H. (1985). *Working with parents: Frameworks for collaboration.* Milton Keynes: Open University Press.

David, M., Edwards, R., Hughes, M., & Ribbens, J. (1993). *Mothers and education: Inside out? Exploring family-education policy and experience.* New York: St Martins Press.

DCSF (Department for Children, Schools and Families). (2007). *The children's plan: Building brighter futures.* London: The Stationary Office.

DES. (1967). *Children and their primary schools (The Plowden report).* London: HMSO.

Desforges, C., & Abouchaar, A. (2003). *The impact of parental involvement, parental support and family education on pupil achievement and adjustment: Research report 433.* London: Department for Education and Skills.

Deslandes, R., & Cloutier, R. (2002). Adolescents' perception of parental involvement in schooling. *School Psychology International, 23*(2), 220–232.

Dinkmeyer, D. C., & Muro, J. J. (1979). *Group counselling: Theory and practice* (2nd ed.). Itasca, IL: Peacock.

Eccles, J. S., & Harold, R. D. (1993). Parent-school involvement during the early adolescent years. *Teachers College Record, 94*(3), 568–587.

Education Review Office. (2008). *Partners in learning: Schools' engagement with parents, whanau and communities.* Wellington: Author.

Edwards, R., & Alldred, P. (2000). A typology of parental involvement in education centering on children and young people: negotiating familialisation, institutionalisation and individualism. *British Journal of Sociology of Education, 21*(3), 435–455.

Egan, G. (1982). *The skilled helper* (2nd ed.). Monterey, CA: Brooks/Cole.

Elias, M. J., Patrikakou, E. N., & Weissberg, R. P. (2007). A competence-based framework for parent-school-community partnerships in secondary schools. *School Psychology International, 28*(5), 540–554.

Epstein, J. L. (2001). *School, family and community partnerships.* Boulder, CO: Westview Press.

Epstein, J. L., & Dauber, S. L. (1991). School programs and teacher practices of parent involvement in inner-city elementary and middle schools. *Elementary School Journal, 91*(3), 289–305.

Epstein, J. L., & Salinas, K. C. (2004). Partnering with families and communities. *Educational Leadership, 61*(8), 12–18.

Fan, X., & Chen, M. (2001). Parent involvement and students' academic achievement: A meta-analysis. *Educational Psychology Review, 13*(1), 1–22.

Featherstone, H. (1981). *A difference in the family.* Harmondsworth: Penguin.

Flanigan, C. B. (2007). Preparing preservice teachers to partner with parents and communities: An analysis of college of education faculty focus groups. *School Community Journal, 17*(2), 89–109.

Gordon, T. (1970). *Parent effectiveness training.* New York: Wyden.

Grant, K. B., & Ray, J. A. (2010). *Home, school and community collaboration: Culturally responsive family involvement.* Los Angeles: Sage.

Green, C. L., Walker, J. M. T., Hoover-Dempsey, K. V., & Sandler, H. M. (2007). Parents' motivations for involvement in children's education: An empirical test of a theoretical model of parental involvement. *Journal of Educational Psychology, 99*(3), 532–544.

Greenwood, G. E., & Hickman, C. W. (1991). Research and practice in parent involvement: Implications for teacher education. *Elementary School Journal, 91*(3), 279–288.

Harding, J., & Pike, G. (1988). *Parental involvement in secondary schools.* London: ILEA Learning Resources Branch.

Harris, A., & Goodall, J. (2008). Do parents know they matter? Engaging all parents in learning. *Educational Research, 50*(3), 277–289.

Harry, B. (1992). *Cultural diversity, families and the special education system: Communication and empowerment.* New York: Teachers College Press.

Hattie, J. (2009). *Visible learning: A synthesis of over 800 meta-analyses relating to achievement.* London: Routledge.

Hayes, D., & Chodkiewicz, A. (2006). School-community links: supporting learning in the middle years. *Research Papers in Education, 21*(1), 3–18.

Hegarty, S. (1993). Home-school relations: A perspective from special education. In P. Munn (Ed.), *Parents and schools: Customers, managers or partners?* (pp. 117–130). London: Routledge.

Henderson, A., & Berla, N. (Eds.). (1994). *A new generation of evidence: The family is critical to student achievement.* Washington, DC: Centre for Law and Education.

Henderson, A. T., & Mapp, K. L. (2002). *A new wave of evidence: The impact of school, family and community connections on student achievement.* Austin, TX: Southwest Educational Development Laboratory.

Henderson, A. T., Mapp, K. L., Johnson, V. R., & Davies, D. (2007). *Beyond the bake sale: The essential guide to family-school partnerships.* New York: The New Press.

Herzog, M. J. R., & Pittman, R. B. (1995). Home, family and community: Ingredients in the rural education equation. *Phi Delta Kappan, 77,* 113–118.

Hill, N. E., Castellino, D. R., Lansford, J. E., Nowlin, P., Dodge, K. A., Bates, J. E., et al. (2004). Parent academic involvement as related to school behaviour, achievement and aspirations: Demographic variations across adolescence. *Child Development, 75*(5), 1491–1509.

Hill, N. E., & Taylor, L. C. (2004). Parental school involvement and children's academic achievement: Pragmatics and issues. *Current Directions in Psychological Science, 13*(4), 161–164.

Holland, S., & Ward, C. (1990). *Assertiveness: A practical approach.* Bicester: Winslow Press.

Hoover-Dempsey, K. V., & Sandler, H. M. (1997). Why do parents become involved in their children's education? *Review of Educational Research, 67*(1), 3–42.

Hoover-Dempsey, K. V., Walker, J. M. T., Sandler, H. M., Whetsel, D., Green, C. L., Wilkins, A. S., et al. (2005). Why do parents become involved? *Elementary School Journal, 106*(2), 105–130.

Hornby, G. (1989). A model for parent participation. *British Journal of Special Education, 16*(4), 161–162.

Hornby, G. (1990). The organisation of parent involvement. *School Organisation, 10*(2), 247–252.

Hornby, G. (1994). *Counselling in child disability.* London: Chapman and Hall.

Hornby, G. (1995). *Working with parents of children with special needs.* London: Cassell.

Hornby, G. (2000). *Improving parental involvement.* London: Cassell.

Hornby, G., Hall, E., & Hall, C. (2003). *Counselling pupils in schools: Skills and strategies for teachers.* London: RoutledgeFalmer.

Hornby, G., & Lafaele, R. (2011). Barriers to parental involvement in education: An explanatory model. *Educational Review, 63*(1), 37–52.

Hornby, G., & Murray, R. (1983). Group programmes for parents of children with various handicaps. *Child: Care, health and development., 9*(3), 185–198.

Hornby, G., & Witte, C. (2010a). Parent involvement in rural elementary schools in New Zealand: A survey. *Journal of Child and Family Studies, 19*(6), 771–777.

Hornby, G., & Witte, C. (2010b). Parent involvement in inclusive primary schools in New Zealand: Implications for improving practice and for teacher education. *International Journal of Whole schooling, 6*(1), 27–38.

Hornby,G. & Witte, C. (2010c). A survey of parental involvement in secondary schools in New Zealand. *School Psychology International, 31*(5), 495–508.

Hornby, G., & Witte, C. (2010d). A Survey of parental involvement in middle schools in New Zealand. *Pastoral Care in Education, 28*(1), 59–69.

Howe, F., & Simmons, B. J. (2005). Nurturing the parent-teacher alliance. *Phi Delta Kappa Fastbacks, 533*, 5–41.

Jeynes, W. H. (2003). A meta-analysis: The effects of parental involvement on minority children's academic achievement. *Education and Urban Society, 35*, 202–218.

Jeynes, W. H. (2005). A meta-analysis of the relation of parental involvement to urban elementary school student academic achievement. *Urban Education, 40*(3), 237–269.

Jeynes, W. H. (2007). The relation between parental involvement and urban secondary school student academic achievement: A meta-analysis. *Urban Education, 42*(1), 82–110.

Jimmerson, S. R., Oakland, T. D., & Farrell, P. T. (2006). *The handbook of international school psychology*. Thousand Oaks, CA: Sage.

Karther, D. E., & Lowden, F. Y. (1997). Fostering effective parent involvement. *Contemporary Education, 69*(1), 41–44.

Kinney, P. (2005). Letting students take the lead. *Principal Leadership, 6*(2), 33–36.

Koki, S., & Lee, H. (1998). Parental involvement in education: What works in the Pacific? Promising practices in the Pacific region. *Eric Digest: ED426835*. Retrieved September 2, 2008 from http://www.eric.ed.gov

Koutrouba, K., Antonopoulou, E., Tsitsas, G., & Zenakou, E. (2009). An investigation of Greek teachers' views on parental involvement in education. *School Psychology International, 30*(3), 311–318.

Kroth, R. L. (1985). *Communicating with parents of exceptional children* (2nd ed.). Denver: Love.

Little, N., & Allan, J. (1989). Student-led teacher parent conferences. *Elementary School Guidance & Counseling, 20*, 277–282.

Lombana, J. H. (1983). *Home-school partnerships: Guidelines and strategies for educators*. New York: Grune & Stratton.

Lueder, D. C. (2000). *Creating partnerships with parents: An educator's guide*. Lanham, MD: Scarecrow Press.

Macbeth, A. (1984). *The child between: A report on school-family relations in the countries of the European Community*: Vol 13. *Education studies series*. Luxembourg: Office for Official Publications of the European Community.

Manthei, M. (1981). *Positively me: A guide to assertive behaviour* (revised edn). Auckland, New Zealand: Methuen.

McConkey, R. (1985). *Working with parents: A practical guide for teachers and therapists*. London: Croom Helm.

MoE. (2005). *The schooling strategy 2005–2010*. Wellington, New Zealand: Ministry of Education.

Montgomery, D. (Ed.). (2009). *Able, gifted and talented underachievers* (2nd ed.). Chichester: Wiley-Blackwell.

Morgan, S. R. (1985). *Children in crisis: A team approach in the schools*. London: Taylor & Francis.

Munn, P. (1993). Introduction. In P. Munn (Ed.), *Parents and schools: Customers, managers or partners?* (pp. 1–10). London: Routledge.

National Council for Accreditation of Teacher Education. (2002). *Professional standards for the accreditation of schools, colleges and departments of education*. Washington, DC: Author.

National Opinion Research Centre. (1997). The study of opportunities for and barriers to family involvement in education: Preliminary results. Survey, University of Chicago, IL. *Eric Digest: ED 414088*. Retrieved October 2, 2007 from http://www.eric.ed.gov

OECD. (1997). *Parents as partners in schooling*. Paris: Centre for Educational Research & Innovative Publications.

Osborne, S., & deOnis, A. (1997). Parent involvement in rural schools: Implications for educators. *Rural Educator, 19*(2), 20–25. 29.

Parsons, C. (1999). *Education, exclusion and citizenship*. London: Routledge.

Pelco, L. E., Ries, R. R., Jacobson, L., & Melka, S. (2000). Perspectives and practices in family-school partnerships: A national survey of school psychologists. *School Psychology Review, 29*(2), 235–250.

Pomerantz, E. M., Moorman, E. A., & Litwack, S. D. (2007). The how, whom and why of parents' involvement in children's academic lives: More is not always better. *Review of Educational Research, 77*(3), 373–410.

Pugh, G., & De'Ath, E. (1984). *The needs of parents: Practice and policy in parent education*. London: Macmillan.

Reay, D. (1998). *Class work: Mothers' involvement in their children's primary schooling*. London: UCL Press.

Rogers, C. R. (1980). *A way of being*. Boston: Houghton Mifflin.

Rosenthal, D. M., & Sawyers, J. Y. (1996). Building successful home/school partnerships. *Childhood Education, 72*(4), 194–200.

Rudney, G. (2005). *Every teacher's guide to working with parents*. Thousand Oaks, CA: Corwin Press.

Sanders, M. (2006). *Building school-community partnerships: Collaboration for student success*. Thousand Oaks, CA: Corwin Press.

Seligman, M. (2000). *Conducting effective conferences with parents of children with disabilities*. New York: Guilford.

Seligman, M., & Darling, R. (2007). *Ordinary families: Special children: A systems approach to childhood disability* (3rd ed.). New York: Guilford.

Sicley, D. (1993). Effective methods of communication: Practical interventions for classroom teachers. *Intervention in School and Clinic, 29*(2), 105–108.

Simpson, R. L. (1996). *Conferencing parents of exceptional children* (3rd ed.). Austin, TX: PRO-ED.

Sonnenschien, P. (1984). Parents and professionals: An uneasy relationship. In M. L. Henninger & E. M. Nesselroad (Eds.), *Working with parents of handicapped children: A book of readings for school personnel* (pp. 129–139). Lanham, MD: University Press of America.

Spera, C. (2005). A review of the relationship among parenting practices, parenting styles and adolescent school achievement. *Educational Psychology Review, 17*(2), 125–146.

Swap, S. M. (1993). *Developing home-school partnerships*. New York: Teachers College Press.

Topping, K. J. (1986). *Parents as educators: Training parents to teach their children*. London: Croom Helm.

Trotzer, J. P. (1977). *The counselor and the Group: Integrating theory, training and practice*. Monterey, CA: Brooks/Cole.

Turnbull, A. P., & Turnbull, H. R. (1986). *Families, professionals and exceptionality*. Columbus, OH: Merrill.

Turnbull, A., Turnbull, R., Erwin, E. J., Soodak, L. C., & Shogren, K. A. (2011). *Families, professionals and exceptionality*. Boston: Pearson.

USDoE. (2001). *No child left behind: Overview*. Washington, DC: United States Department of Education.

Waller, H., & Waller, J. (1998). *Linking home and school: Partnership in practice in primary education*. London: David Fulton.

Wheeler, P. (1992). Promoting parent involvement in secondary schools. *NASSP Bulletin, 76*, 28–35.

Williams, B., Williams, J., & Ullman, A. (2002). *Parental involvement in education: Research report 332*. London: Department for Education and Skills.

Williamson, D. L. (1982). *Group power: How to develop, lead, and help groups achieve goals*. Englewood Cliffs, NJ: Prentice-Hall.

Wolfendale, S. (1983). *Parental participation in the education and development of children.* London: Gordon & Breach.

Wolfendale, S. (Ed.). (1989). *Parental involvement: Developing networks between school, home and community.* London: Cassell.

Wolfendale, S. (1992). *Empowering parents and teachers.* London: Cassell.

Young, S. J. (1991). The involvement of parents in the education of their physically disabled child. Unpublished MEd Thesis, University of Hull.

Young, M. D. (1998). Importance of trust in increasing parental involvement and student achievement in Mexican American communities. *Eric Digest: ED423587.* Retrieved September 2, 2008 from http://www.eric.ed.gov

Index

Lightning Source UK Ltd.
Milton Keynes UK
UKHW022248140120
356913UK00012B/104/P